ANALYZING THE ISSUES

CRITICAL PERSPECTIVES ON
LEGALIZING MARIJUANA

Edited by Anne C. Cunningham

Enslow Publishing

101 W. 23rd Street
Suite 240
New York, NY 10011
USA

enslow.com

Published in 2017 by Enslow Publishing, LLC
101 W. 23rd Street, Suite 240, New York, NY 10011

Library of Congress Cataloging-in-Publication Data

Names: Cunningham, Anne C., editor.
Title: Critical perspectives on legalizing marijuana / edited by Anne C. Cunningham.
Description: New York, NY : Enslow Publishing, 2017. | Series: Analyzing the issues | Includes bibliographical references and index.
Identifiers: LCCN 2015045447 | ISBN 9780766076693 (library bound)
Subjects: LCSH: Drug legalization—United States—Juvenile literature. | Marijuana—Law and legislation—United States—Juvenile literature. | Marijuana—Government policy—United States—Juvenile literature. | Marijuana abuse—United States—Juvenile literature.
Classification: LCC HV5825 .C746 2017 | DDC 362.29/55610973—dc23
LC record available at https://lccn.loc.gov/2015045447

Printed in the United States of America

To Our Readers: We have done our best to make sure all website addresses in this book were active and appropriate when we went to press. However, the author and the publisher have no control over and assume no liability for the material available on those websites or on any websites they may link to. Any comments or suggestions can be sent by e-mail to customerservice@enslow.com.

Excerpts and articles have been reproduced with the permission of the copyright holders.

Photo Credits: Cover, Matthew Micah Wright/Lonely Planet Images Collection/Getty Images (protesters), Thaiview/Shutterstock.com (background, pp. 4–5 background), gbreezy/Shutterstock.com (magnifying glass on spine); p. 4 Ghornstern/Shutterstock.com (header design element, chapter start background throughout book.

CONTENTS

INTRODUCTION

Marijuana has gone mainstream. Once the illicit "jazz cigarette" of the original hipsters of the 1950s, a sacred herb for hippies, and the choice intoxicant of vaguely counter-cultural (though often ethnically coded) entertainers, such as Cheech and Chong, marijuana has largely been stripped of any residual caché. Television, film, and music now routinely represent ordinary people of all races, ages, and walks of life smoking, vaporizing ("vaping"), or otherwise partaking in marijuana consumption. With cheerfully ubiquitous, pun-filled headlines riffing on stoner lingo, news and media outlets eagerly cover each new battle site of the legalization debate—and generally from a pot-positive disposition.

Overwhelming evidence suggests public attitudes are changing in favor of cannabis reform as well. According to national polling by Pew, Gallup, and General Social Survey, Americans are currently more permissive of marijuana use than ever before in our nation's history. The majority of Americans now favor complete legalization of marijuana. This percentage increases significantly when the discussion is limited to medical marijuana. Indeed, unless a drastic reversal of public opinion intervenes, more and more states will continue blazing a trail towards full legality of marijuana for adults over 21. Today, 23 states allow medical marijuana, and Colorado, Oregon, Alaska, Washington, and the District of Columbia have legalized recreational marijuana. It is expected that many more states will follow suit, with ballot measures gaining popularity in California, Vermont, New York, and Nevada.

Although Colorado was the first state to legalize recreational marijuana in 2014, California led the nation in marijuana law reform. In 1996, California voters passed Proposition 215, also called the Compassionate Use Act. This made marijuana legal, provided the user was under the supervision of a primary caregiver. Contrary to popular misconception, a primary caregiver need not be a medical doctor, or even a licensed health care professional. California law defines "primary caregiver" simply as someone responsible for the health, housing, and safety of another person. Despite enacting the will of the state's majority, the Compassionate Use Act was not without its challengers. Conservative counties refused to issue state mandated identification cards protecting medical marijuana patients from arrest. Although the counties lost due to preemption by state law, this was far from the end of legal challenges facing marijuana users.

This is because as far as the federal government is concerned, marijuana remains a Schedule I controlled substance. Although under the Obama administration the Drug Enforcement Agency has pledged not to make marijuana cases a priority, possession and/or use of the drug is nonetheless a federal crime technically subject to prosecution. As we'll see in Chapter Three, this discrepancy has caused much confusion in the courts. These legal issues will likely proliferate until Congress enacts legislation "descheduling" the drug. This issue was high on the political agenda for the 2016 presidential candidates, especially for savvy politicians eager to gain political capital from widespread public support.

Given that legalization is an eventuality, for many experts the question then becomes: how do we best maximize the benefits of legal cannabis such as increased personal liberty, state revenue from taxation, and decreased stress on the legal system, while curtailing negative impacts such as potential increases in addiction rates and abuse by minors? Most experts agree that a for-profit marijuana industry akin to the alcohol and tobacco industries is most definitely not the answer, since their business model depends on market expansion. As we've seen from these industries, profiteering and lobbying power could dramatically increase the negative side of legal cannabis, possibly even to the degree that public costs outstrip the benefits. For many, a powerful, corporatized marijuana industry (sometimes referred to as "big tobacco 2.0") is potentially too high of a price to pay for marginally increased tax revenues and civil liberties.

For those paying attention (and we certainly hope you are!), the challenge of creating new and optimum legal markets for marijuana dovetail nicely with the larger goal of curtailing corporate power relative to government regulatory bodies—a principle with broader implications, to be sure. For example, in the face of climate change, one could argue that fossil fuels pose a far greater risk to public health than marijuana. And while it's too late to ban or criminalize the fossil fuel industry, the failure to intervene and do so during an earlier era is a cautionary tale.

Arguably there are issues of more importance than marijuana, such as income inequality and corporate control of politics, just to name two examples. However, the national conversation regarding cannabis legalization actually encompasses these and other large political and social problems above one's personal feeling for the drug. This is the primary reason why we as citizens should be informed about marijuana reform—from all angles.

CHAPTER 1

WHAT THE EXPERTS SAY

Perhaps the most prevalent argument against legalizing marijuana is the detrimental effects its increased availability and potency will have on both the physiological and psychological development of young people, and particularly adolescents. Robin Murray's "Marijuana and Madness: Clinical Implications of Increased Availability and Potency," the first article in this chapter, predicts increased use will mean more dependence, cognitive impairment, and psychosis. Murray warns that marijuana is far from harmless and can cause numerous, often severe, metal health problems.

Following this dire warning, we'll examine Dr. Curren Warf's response to the American Academy of Pediatrics in regard to their decision to take a stand against marijuana legalization. Warf argues that US drug policy has had a more detrimental effect on America's youth than marijuana use. Dr. Alain Joffe, in response, attempts to refute Warf's claims.

Finally, Mark Kleiman holds that liberalizing public views toward marijuana are driving the legislative process speedily toward legalization. Thus, we should implement policies to increase its benefits while reducing its negative consequences. To Kleiman, a corporatized marijuana industry with lobbying power (as mentioned earlier, this is often called "big tobacco 2.0") is a worst-case scenario. Since the maximization of consumption (and hence profits) runs contrary to public health objectives, experts agree that we should seek alternatives to the capitalist model for the marijuana market whenever possible.

"MARIJUANA AND MADNESS: CLINICAL IMPLICATIONS OF INCREASED AVAILABILITY AND POTENCY," BY ROBIN M. MURRAY, FROM *PSYCHIATRIC TIMES*, APRIL 30, 2015

Attitudes toward cannabis are changing. Uruguay has legalized its use, as have 4 American states; Jamaica is in the process of following suit. In addition, 17 US states have decriminalized cannabis, while 23 others have passed medical marijuana laws.

In many ways, cannabis is similar to alcohol; most of those who use it do so moderately, enjoy it, and suffer few if any adverse effects. However, in a minority of heavy users, problems develop. Given the likelihood that cannabis will become more available, it is important to establish any harms its use may cause so clinicians can identify and treat these. The main psychological harms that have been reported are dependence, cognitive impairment, and psychosis.

WHY DO PEOPLE ENJOY SMOKING CANNABIS?

The cannabis plant produces compounds known as cannabinoids in glandular trichomes, mostly around the flowering tops of the plant. Recreational cannabis is derived from these and has been traditionally available as herb (marijuana, grass, weed) or resin (hashish, hash). The cannabis plant produces more than 70 cannabinoids, but the one responsible for the "high" that users enjoy is tetrahydrocannabinol (THC). This activates the CB1 receptor, part of the endocannabinoid system, which, in turn, affects the dopaminergic reward system that is altered by all drugs of abuse.

Psychological dependence and tolerance can occur with cannabis. It remains in the body for several weeks, so withdrawal is very gradual but anxiety, insomnia, appetite disturbance, and depression can develop. Some reports claim that in 10% of persons who use cannabis and in 25% of daily users, dependence develops. (1) Cannabis dependence is an increasingly common reason why patients seek help from drug treatment clinics.

COGNITIVE IMPAIRMENT

Many studies implicate adolescent cannabis use with poor subsequent educational achievement. Silins and colleagues (2) observed more than 2,500 young people in Australia and New Zealand. Their findings suggest that daily cannabis use before age 17 was associated with "clear reductions" in the likelihood of completing high school and obtaining a university degree.

THC disrupts the function of the hippocampus, a structure crucial to memory, and when it is given to volunteers, transient cognitive impairment is seen. Such impairment likely is why drivers under the influence of cannabis are at double the risk for traffic accidents. (2) Long-term users show more obvious deficits, but questions remain about what happens when they stop. Some studies suggest they can recover fully, while others indicate that only partial recovery is possible. (3)

RISK OF PSYCHOSIS

It has long been known that persons with schizophrenia are more likely to smoke cannabis than is the rest of the population. Until recently, the general view was that they must be smoking to self-medicate or otherwise help them to cope with their illness. If this were so, then one might expect psychotic cannabis users to have a better outcome than nonusers. However, the opposite is the case; the patients who continue to use cannabis are much more likely to continue to have delusions and hallucinations. (4)

However, this does not prove that cannabis use causes the poor outcomes. The possible causal role of cannabis can only be answered by prospective epidemio-logical studies. In the first of these, 45,750 young men were asked about their drug use when they were conscripted into the Swedish army. (5) Those who had used cannabis more than 50 times when conscripted, were 6 times more likely to receive a diagnosis of schizophrenia over the next 15 years. Since 2002, a series of prospective studies have confirmed that individuals who used cannabis at the baseline evaluation had a greater risk of subsequently developing psychotic symptoms or full-blown schizo-phrenia than non-users. (4-7)

Some skeptics have suggested that perhaps those who are predisposed to schizophrenia are especially likely to use cannabis. However, in the Dunedin birth cohort study, the subjects were intensively studied since childhood, so those who had already appeared psycho-sis-prone at age 11 were excluded. (6) The researchers found a link between cannabis use and later schizo-phrenia, even when the effects of other drugs known to increase risk of psychosis were excluded. Another criticism was that some individuals might have been using cannabis in an attempt to ameliorate symptoms of psychosis or its precursors. However, a second New Zealand study, this time from Christchurch, showed that once minor psychotic symptoms developed, individuals tended to smoke less. (7)

Anyone familiar with the effects of alcohol would immediately accept that the frequency of drinking is rele-vant to its adverse effects. The same is true with cannabis; long-term daily users are most at risk. Nevertheless, the majority of daily users will not become psychotic. Indeed, when a young man in whom schizophrenia has developed after years of smoking cannabis is asked whether he thinks his habit may have contributed to the disorder, he might answer, "No, my friends smoke as much as I do, and they're fine." It seems that some people are especially vulnerable.

Individuals with a paranoid personality are at greatest risk, along with those who have a family history of psychosis. Inheriting certain variants of genes that influence the dopamine system, which is implicated in psychosis, may also make some users especially susceptible; examples include AKT1, DRD2, and possibly COMT. (8, 9)

CHANGES IN POTENCY

In 1845, French psychiatrist Jacques-Joseph Moreau used cannabis and gave it to some of his students and patients. He concluded that cannabis could precipitate "acute psychotic reactions, generally lasting but a few hours, but occasionally as long as a week." (10) Modern experimental studies confirm that intravenous administration of THC in healthy volunteers can produce acute psychotic symptoms in a dose-dependent manner. (8)

The proportion of THC in traditional marijuana and resin in the 1960s was approximately 1% to 3%. Potency began to rise in the 1980s, when cannabis growers such as David Watson, commonly known as "Sam the Skunkman," fled the Reagan-inspired "War on Drugs" and brought cannabis seeds to Amsterdam, where cannabis could be sold legally in "coffee shops." Together with Dutch enthusiasts, they bred more potent plants, setting the scene for a slow but steady increase in new varieties of marijuana, including sensimilla (often called "skunk" because of its strong smell) harvested from unpollinated female flowers. The proportion of THC in sensimilla has risen to between 16% and 20% in England and Holland, respectively, and high-potency varieties have taken over much of the traditional market (9,11); the same trend, although lagging a few years behind, has occurred in the US. (12)

Traditional cannabis often contained not only THC but an equivalent amount of cannabinol. This has been shown in experimental studies to ameliorate the psychotomimetic effects of THC, and possibly to have antipsychotic properties. (13) However, plants bred to produce a high concentration of THC cannot also produce much cannabinol, so the high THC types of cannabis contain little or no cannabinol. Such varieties are more psychotogenic; one study showed that persons who used high-THC-low-cannabinol cannabis on a daily basis were 5 times more likely than non-users to suffer from a psychotic disorder. (14) Another study that tested hair for cannabinoids showed that users with both detectable THC and cannabinol in their hair had fewer psychotic symptoms than those with only THC. (15)

The increasing availability of high-potency cannabis explains why psychiatrists are more concerned about cannabis now than they were in the 1960s and 1970s. The trend toward greater potency continues: new forms of resin oil reportedly contain up to 60% of THC. (11) These very potent forms remain unusual, but synthetic cannabinoids, often termed "spice" or "K2," are now commonly advertised and sold on Web sites that keep within the law by labeling their products as incense—or adding "not for human consumption." While THC only partially activates the CB1 receptor, most spice/ K2 molecules fully activate the receptor and, consequently, acute adverse reactions are more common. A survey of 80,000 drug users showed that those who used synthetic cannabinoids were 30 times more likely to end up in an emergency department than users of traditional cannabis. (16)

CANNABIS AND THE DEVELOPING BRAIN

It seems that starting cannabis use in early adolescence increases the likelihood of problems. For example, in the Dunedin study, those starting at 18 years or later showed only a non-significant increase in the risk of psychosis by age 26, but among those starting at age 15 or earlier, risk was increased 4-fold. (6)

Those starting cannabis use early also appear more likely to develop cognitive impairment. Pope and colleagues (17) found that long-term heavy cannabis users who began smoking before age 17 had lower verbal IQ scores than those who began smoking at age 17 or older. Meier and colleagues (18) followed a birth cohort in Dunedin, New Zealand, up to age 38 years. Their findings suggest that persistent cannabis use over several decades causes a decline of up to 8 points in IQ; such dramatic findings need to be replicated before they can be accepted.

The results from animal studies also show that THC administration produces a greater effect on cognitive function in juvenile rats than in adult rats. Moreover, imaging studies in persons with long-term, very heavy cannabis use indicate detectable brain changes, especially in those who started smoking in adolescence. (19) Although the studies remain contentious, a possible explanation is that beginning cannabis use at an age when the brain is still developing might permanently impair the endocannabinoid system; this may affect other neurotransmitters, such as dopamine—known to be implicated in both learning and in psychosis.

IMPLICATIONS

Cannabis is now generally recognized as a contributory cause of schizophrenia. Although psychosis develops in only a small minority of cannabis users, when you consider that almost 200 million people worldwide use cannabis, the number of people who suffer cannabis-induced psychosis is likely to be in the millions, and the impact on mental health services is significant. The proportion of psychosis that has been attributed to cannabis use in different countries ranges from 8% to 24%, depending, in part, on the prevalence of use and the potency of the cannabis. (20)

Politicians have the difficult job of balancing the enjoyment that many people get from cannabis against the harm that afflicts some people. Furthermore, cannabis can alleviate chronic pain or symptoms associated with chemotherapy. Medical marijuana may be largely a cover used by the increasingly powerful marijuana industry to introduce recreational use, but research into the numerous components of cannabis should be encouraged, since it may produce drugs with important therapeutic uses.

Current trends are toward relaxing laws on cannabis, but no one knows the likely outcome. Will legalization mean an increase in consumption? Early reports from Colorado and Washington suggest an increase. Will this have knock-on effects on use by those in their early teens who seem most susceptible to adverse effects? Will the mental health and addiction services be able to cope? How effective will educational campaigns regarding the risks of regular use of high-potency cannabis or synthetic cannabinoids be? Might a simple genetic test reveal who is most likely to suffer adverse mental effects?

Many questions remain to be answered. In the meantime, as cannabis use continues to win acceptance, psychiatrists are likely to see more of the casualties.

1. What evidence does the author use to substantiate the article's claims? Do you find this method incomplete? Why or why not?

2. Does increased potency mean increased total THC consumption? Wouldn't most users simply consume less?

"RESPONSE TO THE AMERICAN ACADEMY OF PEDIATRICS REPORT ON LEGALIZATION OF MARIJUANA," BY CURREN WARF AND ALAIN JOFFE, FROM *PEDIATRICS*, NOVEMBER 2005

To the Editor,

It is unfortunate and somewhat puzzling that the American Academy of Pediatrics (AAP) has chosen this time to take a stand against the legalization of marijuana. (1) Many of the arguments for and against legalization, or decriminalization, are noted in their technical report, although several dimensions should be explored more thoroughly. The editors of *The Lancet* are quoted as saying that "cannabis per se is not a hazard to society but driving it further underground may well be." (2) When one advocates against legalization, the real intent is to advocate for establishing criminal records and imprisonment for young people and adults for a common exploratory behavior. Those who advocate for prosecution as a felony are advocating for 1-year prison sentences for marijuana possession and, in some circumstances, loss of voting rights. In view of the widespread use of marijuana, any enforcement of the law is inevitably capricious and inequitable. It is clear that what we do to people for using marijuana may be far worse than any biomedical consequences of using the drug.

The United States now has 25% of the world's incarcerated population, well over 2 million individuals, 80% of whom were arrested on a drug-related offense. Young people with records are stigmatized for employment and professional education. Incarcerating young people takes them out of their normative social development and exposes them to grave physical danger and an inherently pathologic social environment. Irrational drug laws are the underpinning for much of this mass incarceration. It seems that the real harm related to marijuana use is not so much any purported physical or psychological impairments as it is what we as a society do to marijuana users.

The unshakable determination of the federal government to continue classifying marijuana as a schedule I narcotic, equating it with heroin in its level of danger, is laughable on its face but emblematic of the irrationality of the drug laws far more than the danger of the drug itself. Not only does it prevent the exploration of marijuana for medical uses, but it also provides a legal basis for harsh penalties for use and sale.

As is acknowledged in the AAP technical report, marijuana is of far less danger than either alcohol or tobacco. In the early part of the last century, America experimented with prohibition, making alcohol illegal, in part because of the social destructiveness of alcoholism in our society. The result was not only an actual increase in alcoholism but, more significantly, the monopolization of the alcohol market by organized crime and the explosion of violence regarding its marketing and sale. Prohibition was more socially destructive than alcoholism. The federal government finally relented, but only after many people paid with their lives and reputations for this experiment. Similarly, the result of drugs being illegal is that organizations that are involved in the transportation and sale of these drugs operate outside the law.

One should also consider the practical obstacles to a successful policy of having the marijuana plant illegal. It is, after all, a weed that grows easily in essentially any temperate climate. It is used by tens of millions of Americans and is reputed to be a major cash crop, albeit an illegal one, in a number of states. Any enforcement of drug laws under these circumstances is unavoidably haphazard, arbitrary, and discriminatory, not to mention unsuccessful. These are some of the reasons why the criminalization of marijuana has been such an abject failure.

The argument of potential long-term consequences of marijuana use has gone on inconclusively for years and will probably go on for many more. As noted in the article, use and perceived risk of marijuana has been cyclical, but as we all know, tens of millions of Americans have used it at some point in their lives, including many physicians (not to mention pediatricians and adolescent medicine specialists), politicians, academics, business leaders, attorneys, judges, and others. I am hard pressed to say that from any reasonable standpoint it has had a peculiarly deleterious affect. By the same token, one can argue that wine ingestion can lead to addiction and many other short-term and long-term problems, but I have been to many professional conferences, including pediatric conferences, at which wine was provided. And although cigarettes are not illegal, I know more than one pediatrician who secretly smokes.

No one advocates for adolescents to use marijuana, wine, or tobacco, but we also know that millions of adolescents actually do use them, not to mention college youth and young working people. Whether we like it or not, it is part of the exploratory and experimental behaviors in which many, if not most, adolescents in our culture engage. Given a safe environment and appropriate adult role models, most young people are able to moderate their use of intoxicants fairly well most of the time. All of these young people need to learn how to negotiate through a world in which drugs, alcohol, and tobacco exist and will not disappear because physicians disapprove of them. The illegal status of marijuana means that many of these young people come into contact with people who sell other, more dangerous drugs and, in the course of purchasing marijuana, expose themselves to the very real risk of becoming involved in more serious drug use.

It is hard enough to grow up in America. Inevitably, young people will feel that the hypocrisy so evident in the double standard that accepts the legality of alcohol and cigarettes for their parent's generation but criminalizes marijuana with dubious arguments will only alienate them further.

I find it disappointing that the AAP has taken the low road on this issue. The medical profession, and the AAP especially, should be a voice for rationality and, yes, courage and be willing to challenge the irrationality of drug laws that have made so many young people pay such a needless price. As noted in their technical report, a survey in 1995 found that among AAP fellows, 18% favored legalization, 24% felt that penalties should be reduced or eliminated, 31% felt it should be available by prescription for medical purposes, and only 26% agreed that it should be a felony. Three quarters of AAP fellows evidently feel that the laws should be liberalized significantly. One has to wonder if people who think that marijuana possession should be a felony have really thought about what this means: do they really think that young people should receive at least 1 year in prison for marijuana-related offenses? Do they really think they should lose their voting rights? What could these people possibly have in mind?

It was only last year that an associate of mine, having successfully completed his PhD and professional boards, had a 4-year delay of licensure in his field solely because he had admitted to a single arrest for marijuana possession as a teenager. Finally, after undergoing monthly drug testing and repeated board hearings, he received his license.

There is something bizarre about the level of scrutiny and our response to marijuana use.

Our drug policies and the policies of the AAP should be driven by rational arguments, looking at material consequences. The AAP needs to gain the courage to challenge the irrationality of federal drug policy and shine a spotlight on its effects on young people.

CURREN WARF, MD, FAAP, FSAM
Division of Adolescent Medicine
Childrens Hospital Los Angeles Los Angeles, CA 90027

In Reply,

Dr Warf states that "[w]hen one advocates against legalization, the real intent is to advocate for establishing criminal records and imprisonment for young people and adults for a common exploratory behavior." Nowhere in our statement did we advocate for such positions. As stated in the technical report, legalization of marijuana would fundamentally change its status in the United

States. The legal status of alcohol and tobacco for adults permits, despite legal sanctions against sales to minors and industry protestations to the contrary, aggressive promotion and sales of these products to young people. The result is that alcohol and tobacco are the 2 drugs most commonly abused by adolescents. Dr Warf seems not to be concerned that use of marijuana by adolescents might well approach similar levels were it also to be legalized.

Implicit in Dr Warf's comments about incarceration is that many individuals wind up in jail for the sale or possession of small quantities of marijuana. We were unable to identify any data to support this position, and Dr Warf provides no data of his own. Again, to oppose legalization is not to endorse incarceration. Similarly, our technical report specifically mentioned support by the American Academy of Pediatrics for additional research into the role of cannabinoids for medical purposes.

We do agree that "tens of millions of Americans have used it [marijuana] at some point in their lives," but our concern is with adolescents, especially young adolescents. Marijuana is much more potent now than it was in the 1960s and 1970s, which is one explanation for why cannabis-use disorders in the United States have increased over the last 10 years. (1) New research on brain development clearly demonstrates that the adolescent brain, which is still developing, is particularly vulnerable to the ill effects of substance abuse, including marijuana. (2,3) Just as early-onset alcohol users are at greater risk for problems later in life, so too young adolescents seem to be at particular risk for numerous negative psychosocial consequences from using marijuana. (4,5) In addition, several large longitudinal studies have demonstrated a link between marijuana use during adolescence and later development of mood disorders and schizophrenia. (6-8) Those who advocate for legalization of marijuana must set forth how they would protect young people in such an environment.

We believe that our technical report was rational and balanced and was based on the best data available to date. Since its publication, evidence has continued to accrue that marijuana is not the harmless drug many wish it were.

ALAIN JOFFE, MD, MPH, FAAP, FOR THE COMMITTEES ON SUBSTANCE ABUSE AND
ADOLESCENCE
Chair, Committee on Substance Abuse
Student Health and Wellness Center Johns Hopkins University Baltimore, MD 21218

1. What are the main reasons why the AAP opposes legalization?

2. Which of the above letters is more convincing, and why?

"HOW NOT TO MAKE A HASH OUT OF CANNABIS LEGALIZATION," BY MARK KLEIMAN, FROM *WASHINGTON MONTHLY*, MARCH/APRIL/MAY 2014

A majority of Americans, and an overwhelming majority of those under thirty, now support the legalization of marijuana. This change in public opinion, which has been building for years but has accelerated of late, is now generating policy changes.

In 2012, voters in Colorado and Washington State endorsed initiatives legalizing not just the use of cannabis but also its commercial production and sale to anyone over the age of twenty-one. That goes further than the "medical marijuana" provisions that are now the law in twenty states. Nonmedical retail sales started on January 1 in Colorado and will begin in early summer in Washington. Similar propositions are likely to be on the ballot in 2014 and 2016 in as many as a dozen other states, including Alaska, Arizona, California, Nevada, and Oregon, and a legalization bill just narrowly passed in the New Hampshire House of Representatives, the first time either chamber of any state legislature has voted for such a bill. Unless something happens to reverse the trend in public opinion, it seems more likely than not that the federal law will change to make cannabis legally available at some point in the next two decades.

The state-by-state approach has generated some happy talk from both advocates and some neutral observers; Justice Louis Brandeis's praise for states as the "laboratories of democracy" has been widely quoted.

Given how much we don't know about the consequences of legalization, there's a reasonable case for starting somewhere, rather than everywhere. Even some who oppose legalization are moderately comforted by the fact that the federal government isn't driving the process. "It's best that this be done state by state," said Pat Buchanan recently on *The McLaughlin Group*, "so you can have a national backlash if it doesn't work out."

But letting legalization unfold state by state, with the federal government a mostly helpless bystander, risks creating a monstrosity; Dr. Frankenstein also had a laboratory. Right now, officials in Washington and Colorado are busy issuing state licenses to cannabis growers and retailers to do things that remain drug-dealing felonies under federal law. The Justice Department could have shut down the process by going after all the license applicants. But doing so would have run the risk of having the two states drop their own enforcement efforts and challenge the feds to do the job alone, something the DEA simply doesn't have the bodies to handle: Washington and Colorado alone have about four times as many state and local police as there are DEA agents worldwide. Faced with that risk, and with its statutory obligation to cooperate with the states on drug enforcement, Justice chose accommodation.

In August, the deputy U.S. attorney general issued a formal—though nonbinding—assurance that the feds would take a mostly hands-off approach. The memo says that as long as state governments pursue "strong and effective" regulation to prevent activities such as distribution to minors, dealing by gangs and cartels, dealing other drugs, selling across state lines, possession of weapons and use of violence, and drugged driving, and as long as marijuana growing and selling doesn't take place on public lands or federal property, enforcement against state-licensed cannabis activity will rank low on the federal priority list. Justice has even announced that it is working with the Treasury Department to reinterpret the banking laws to allow state-licensed cannabis businesses to have checking accounts and take credit cards, avoiding the robbery risks incident to all-cash businesses.

That leaves the brand-new cannabis businesses in Colorado and Washington in statutory limbo. They're quasi-pseudo-hemi-demi-legal: permitted under state law, but forbidden under a federal law that might not be enforced—until, say, the inauguration of President Huckabee, at which point growers and vendors, as well as their lawyers, accountants, and bankers, could go to prison for the things they're doing openly today.

But even if the federal-state legal issues get resolved, the state-level tax and regulation systems likely to emerge will be far from ideal. While they will probably do a good job of eliminating the illicit cannabis markets in those states, they'll be mediocre to lousy at preventing an upsurge of drug abuse as cheap, quality-tested, easily available legal pot replaces the more expensive, unreliable, and harder-to-find material the black market offers.

The systems being put into place in Washington and Colorado roughly resemble those imposed on alcohol after Prohibition ended in 1933. A set of competitive commercial enterprises produce the pot, and a set of competitive commercial enterprises sell it, under modest regulations: a limited number of licenses, no direct sales to minors, no marketing obviously directed at minors, purity/potency testing and labeling, security rules. The post-Prohibition restrictions on alcohol worked reasonably well for a while, but have been substantially undermined over the years as the beer and liquor industries consolidated and used their economies of scale to lower production costs and their lobbying muscle to loosen regulations and keep taxes low (see Tim Heffernan, "Last Call").

The same will likely happen with cannabis. As more and more states begin to legalize marijuana over the next few years, the cannabis industry will begin to get richer—and that means it will start to wield considerably more political power, not only over the states but over national policy, too.

That's how we could get locked into a bad system in which the primary downside of legalizing pot—increased drug abuse, especially by minors—will be greater than it needs to be, and the benefits, including tax revenues, smaller than they could be. It's easy to imagine the cannabis equivalent of an Anheuser-Busch InBev peddling low-cost, high-octane cannabis in Super Bowl commercials. We can do better than that, but only if Congress takes action—and soon.

The standard framing of the cannabis legalization debate is simple: either you're for it or you're against it. Setting up the debate that way tempts proponents of legalization to deny all risks, while supporters of the status quo deny how bad the current situation is. Both sides deny the unknown. In truth, there's no way to gauge all the consequences of adopting unprecedented policies, so it's foolish to pretend to be 100 percent certain of anything. But it's possible to guess in advance some of the categories of gain and loss from policy change, even if the magnitudes are unknown, and to identify the complete wild cards: things that might get either better or worse.

The undeniable gains from legalization consist mostly of getting rid of the damage done by prohibition. (Indeed, as E. J. Dionne and William Galston have pointed out, polling suggests that support for legalization is driven more by discontent with prohibition than by enthusiasm for pot.) Right now, Americans spend about $35 billion a year on illegal cannabis. That money goes untaxed; the people working in the industry aren't gaining legitimate job experience or getting Social Security credit, and some of them spend time behind bars and wind up with felony criminal records. About 650,000 users a year get arrested for possession, something much more likely to happen to a black user than a white one.

We also spend about $1 billion annually in public money keeping roughly 40,000 growers and dealers behind bars at any one time. That's a small chunk of the incarceration problem, but it represents a lot of money and a lot of suffering. The enforcement effort, including the use of "dynamic entry" raids, imposes additional costs in money, liberty, police-community conflict, and, occasionally, lives. Cannabis dealing and enforcement don't contribute much to drug-related violence in the United States, but they make up a noticeable part of Mexico's problems.

Another gain from legalization would be to move the millions of Americans whose crimes begin and end with using illegal cannabis from the wrong side of the law to the right one, bringing an array of benefits to them and their communities in the form of a healthier relationship with the legal and political systems. Current cannabis users, and the millions of others who might choose to start using cannabis if the drug became legal, would also enjoy an increase in personal liberty and be able to pursue, without the fear of legal consequences, what is for most of them a harmless source of pleasure, comfort, relaxation, sociability, healing, creativity, or inspiration. For those people, legalization would also bring with it all the ordinary gains consumers derive from open competition: lower prices, easier access, and a wider range of available products and means of administration, held to quality standards the illicit market can't enforce.

To those real gains must be added the political lure of public revenue that comes without raising taxes on currently legal products or incomes. The revenue take could be substantial: legal production and distribution of the amount of cannabis now sold in the U.S. wouldn't cost more than 20 percent of the $35 billion now being paid for it. If prices were kept high and virtually all of the surplus were captured by taxation, it's possible that cannabis taxation could yield as much as $20 billion per year—around 1 percent of the revenues of all the state governments. Those are, of course, two big ifs. The current pricing and tax systems in Colorado and Washington, which between them account for about 5 percent of national cannabis use, won't give taxpayers there anything resembling the $1 billion a year that would be their prorated share of that hypothetical $20 billion.

So much for the upside. What about the downside?

The losses from legalization would mainly accrue to the minority of consumers who lose control of their cannabis use. About a quarter of the 1600 million Americans who report having used cannabis in the past month say they used it every day or almost every day. Those frequent users also use more cannabis per day of use than do less frequent users. About half of the daily- and near-daily-use population meets diagnostic criteria for substance abuse or dependence—that is, they find that their cannabis habit is interfering with other activities and bringing negative consequences, and that their attempts to cut back on the frequency or quantity of their cannabis use have failed. (Those estimates are based on users' own responses to surveys, so they probably underestimate the actual risks.)

And then, of course, there are the extreme cases. A substantial number of these daily users spend virtually every waking hour under the influence. Legal availability is likely to add both to their numbers and to the intensity of their problems. Jonathan Caulkins has done a calculation suggesting that legalization at low prices might increase the amount of time spent stoned by about 15 billion person-hours per year, concentrated among frequent heavy users rather than among the more numerous Saturday-night partiers. Every year, hundreds of thousands of cannabis users visit emergency departments having unintentionally overdosed, experiencing anxiety, dysphoria, and sometimes panic. Presumably many others suffer very unpleasant experiences without seeking professional attention.

While a bad cannabis habit usually isn't nearly as destructive as a bad alcohol habit, it's plenty bad enough if it happens to you, or to your child or your sibling or your spouse or your parent.

Maybe you think the gains of legalizing marijuana will outweigh the costs; maybe you don't. But that's quickly becoming a moot point. Like it or not, legalization is on its way, unless something occurs to reverse the current trend in public opinion. In any case, it shouldn't be controversial to say that, if we are to legalize cannabis, the policy aim going forward should be to maximize the gains and minimize the disadvantages. But the systems being put in place in Colorado and Washington aren't well designed for that purpose, because they create a cannabis industry whose commercial interest is precisely opposite to the public interest.

Cannabis consumption, like alcohol consumption, follows the so-called 80/20 rule (sometimes called "Pareto's Law"): 20 percent of the users account for 80 percent of the volume. So from the perspective of cannabis vendors, drug abuse isn't the problem; it's the target demographic. Since we can expect the legal cannabis industry to be financially dependent on dependent consumers, we can also expect that the industry's marketing practices and lobbying agenda will be dedicated to creating and sustaining problem drug use patterns.

The trick to legalizing marijuana, then, is to keep at bay the logic of the market—its tendency to create and exploit people with substance abuse disorders. So far, the state-by-state, initiative-driven process doesn't seem up to that challenge. Neither the taxes nor the regulations will prevent substantial decreases in retail prices, which matter much more to very heavy users and to cash-constrained teenagers than they do to casual users. The industry's marketing efforts will be constrained only by rules against appealing explicitly to minors (rules that haven't kept the beer companies from sponsoring Extreme Fighting on television). And there's no guarantee that other states won't create even looser systems. In Oregon, a proposition on the 2012 ballot that was narrowly defeated (53 percent to 47 percent) would have mandated that five of the seven members of the commission to regulate the cannabis industry be chosen by the growers—industry capture, in other words, was written into the proposed law. It remains to be seen whether even the modest taxes and restrictions passed by the voters survive the inevitable industry pressure to weaken them legislatively.

There are three main policy levers that could check cannabis abuse while making the drug legally available. The first and most obvious is price. Roughly speaking, high-potency pot on the illegal market today costs about $10 to $15 per gram. (It's cheaper in the medical outlets in Colorado and Washington.) A joint, enough to get an occasional user stoned more than once, contains about four-tenths of a gram; that much cannabis costs about $5 at current prices. The price in Amsterdam, where retailing is tolerated but growing is still seriously illegal, is about the same, which helps explain why Dutch use hasn't exploded under quasi-legalization. If we too want to avoid a vast increase in heavy cannabis use under legalization, we should create policies to keep the price of the drug about where it is now.

The difficulty is that marijuana is both relatively cheap compared to other drugs and also easy to grow (thus the nickname "weed"), and will just get cheaper and easier to grow under legalization. According to RAND, legal production costs would be a small fraction of the current level, making the pre-tax value of the cannabis in a legally produced joint pennies rather than dollars.

Taxes are one way to keep prices up. But those taxes would have to be ferociously high, and they'd have to be determined by the ounce of pot or (better) by the gram of THC, as alcohol taxes now are, not as a percentage of retail price like a sales tax. Both Colorado and Washington have percentage-of-price taxes, which will fall along with market prices. In states where it was legal, cannabis taxes would have to be more than $200 an ounce to keep prices at current levels; no ballot measure now under consideration has taxes nearly that high.

Collecting such taxes wouldn't be easy in the face of interstate smuggling, as the tobacco markets illustrate. The total taxes on a pack of cigarettes in New York City run about $8 more than the taxes on the same pack in Virginia. Lo and behold, there's a massive illicit industry smuggling cigarettes north, with more than a third of the cigarettes sold in New York escaping New York taxes. Without federal intervention, interstate smuggling of cannabis would be even worse. Whichever state had the lowest cannabis taxes would effectively set prices for the whole country, and the supposed state option to keep the drug illegal would fall victim to inflows from neighboring states.

The other way to keep legal pot prices up is to limit supply. Colorado and Washington both plan to impose production limits on growers. If those limits were kept tight enough, scarcity would lead to a run-up in price. (That's happening right now in Colorado; prices in the limited number of commercial outlets open on January 1 were about 50 percent higher than prices in the medical outlets.) But those states are handing out production rights for modest fixed licensing fees, so any gain from scarcity pricing will go to the industry and encourage even more vigorous marketing. If, instead, production quotas were put up for auction, the gain could go to the taxpayers. Just as a cap-and-trade system for carbon emissions can be made to mimic the effects of a carbon tax, production quotas with an auction would be the equivalent of taxes.

The second policy lever government has is information: it can require or provide product labeling, point-of-sale communication, and outreach to prevent both drug abuse and impaired driving. In principle, posting information about, say, the known chemical composition of one type of cannabis versus another could help consumers use the drug more safely. How that plays out in practice depends on the details of policy design. Colorado and Washington require testing and labeling for chemical content, but techniques for helping consumers translate those numbers into safer consumption practices remain to be developed. The fact that more than 60 percent of cannabis user-days involve people with no more than a high school education creates an additional challenge, one often ignored by the advanced-degree holders who dominate the debate.

The government could also make sure consumers are able to get high-quality information and advice from cannabis vendors. In Uruguay, for example, which is now legalizing on the national level, the current proposal requires cannabis vendors to be registered pharmacists. Cannabis is, after all, a somewhat dangerous drug, and both much more complex chemically and less familiar culturally than beer or wine. In Washington and Colorado, by contrast, the person behind the counter will simply be a sales agent, with no required training about the pharmacology of cannabis and no professional obligation to promote safe use.

A more radical approach would be to enhance consumers' capacity to manage their own drug use with a program of user-determined periodic purchase limits. (See "A Nudge Toward Temperance.")

All of these attempts by government to use information to limit abuse, however, could be overwhelmed by the determined marketing efforts of a deep-pocketed marijuana industry. And the courts' creation of a legal category called "commercial free speech" radically limits attempts to rein in those marketing efforts (see Haley Sweetland Edwards, "The Corporate 'Free Speech' Racket"). The "commercial free speech" doctrine creates an absurd situation: both state governments and the federal government can constitutionally put people in prison for growing and selling cannabis, but they're constitutionally barred from legalizing cannabis with any sort of marketing restriction designed to prevent problem use.

Availability represents a third policy lever. Where can marijuana be sold? During what hours? In what form? There's a reason why stores put candy in the front by the checkout counters; impulse buying is a powerful phenomenon. The more restrictive the rules on marijuana, the fewer new people will start smoking and the fewer new cases of abuse we'll have. Colorado and Washington limit marijuana sales to government-licensed pot stores that have to abide by certain restrictions, such as not selling alcohol and not being located near schools. But they're free to advertise. And there's nothing to keep other states, or Colorado and Washington a few years from now, from allowing pot in any form to be sold in grocery stores or at the 7-Eleven. (Two years before legalizing cannabis, Washington's voters approved a Costco-sponsored initiative to break the state monopoly on sales of distilled spirits.)

To avoid getting locked into bad policies, lawmakers in Washington need to act, and quickly. I know it's hard to imagine anything good coming out of the current Congress, but there's no real alternative.

What's needed is federal legislation requiring states that legalize cannabis to structure their pot markets such that they won't get captured by commercial interests. There are any number of ways to do that, so the legislation wouldn't have to be overly prescriptive. States could, for instance, allow marijuana to be sold only through nonprofit outlets, or distributed via small consumer-owned co-ops (see Jonathan P. Caulkins, "Nonprofit Motive"). The most effective way, however, would be through a system of state-run retail stores.

There's plenty of precedent for this: states from Utah to Pennsylvania to Alabama restrict hard liquor sales to state operated or state-controlled outlets. Such "ABC" ("alcoholic beverage control") stores date back to the end of Prohibition, and operationally they work fine. Similar "pot control" stores could work fine for marijuana, too. A "state store" system would also allow the states to control the pot supply chain. By contracting with many small growers, rather than a few giant ones, states could check the industry's political power (concentrated industries are almost always more effective at lobbying than those comprised of many small companies) and maintain consumer choice by avoiding a beer-like oligopoly offering virtually interchangeable products.

States could also insist that the private growers sign contracts forbidding them from marketing to the public. Imposing that rule as part of a vendor agreement rather than as a regulation might avoid the "commercial free speech" issue, thus eliminating the specter of manipulative marijuana advertising filling the airwaves and covering highway billboards. To prevent interstate smuggling, the federal government should do what it has failed to do with cigarettes: mandate a minimum retail price.

Of course, there's a danger that states themselves, hungry for tax dollars, could abuse their monopoly power over pot, just as they have with state lotteries. To avert that outcome, states should avoid the mistake they made with lotteries: housing them in state revenue departments, which focus on maximizing state income. Instead, the new marijuana control programs should reside in state health departments and be overseen by boards with a majority of health care and substance-abuse professionals. Politicians eager for revenue might still press for higher pot sales than would be good for public health, but they'd at least have to fight a resistant bureaucracy.

How could the federal government get the states to structure their pot markets in ways like these? By giving a new twist to a tried-and-true tool that the Obama administration has wielded particularly effectively: the policy waiver. The federal government would recognize the legal status of cannabis under a state system—making the activities permitted under that system actually legal, not merely tolerated, under federal law—only if the state system contained adequate controls to protect public health and safety, as determined by the attorney general and the secretary of the department of health and human services. That would change the politics of legalization at the state level, with legalization advocates and the cannabis industry supporting tight controls in order to get, and keep, the all-important waiver. Then we would see the laboratories of democracy doing some serious experimentation.

Could such a plan garner enough support in Washington to become law? Certainly not now, given a dysfunctional Congress, an administration with no taste for engaging one more culture war issue, and in the absence of a powerful national organization with a nuanced view of cannabis policy and the muscle to make that view politically salient. But there is a mutually beneficial deal waiting to be made. Though legalization has made headway in states with strong initiative provisions in their constitutions, it's been slow going in other states in which legalization has to go through the legislature, where anti-pot law enforcement groups can easily block it. So it could be many years before legalization reaches the rest of the country or gets formal federal approval that removes the stigma of (even unpunished) lawbreaking from cannabis users. Rather than wait, legalization advocates might be willing to accept something short of full commercialization; some of them actually prefer a noncommercial system. Meanwhile, those who have been opponents of legalization heretofore might—with the writing now on the wall—decide that a tightly regulated and potentially reversible system of legal availability is the least-bad outcome available.

The current political situation seems anomalous. Public opinion continues to move against cannabis prohibition, but no national-level figure of any standing is willing to speak out for change. That's unlikely to last. Soon enough, candidates for president are going to be asked their positions on marijuana legalization. They're going to need a good answer. I suggest something like this: "I'm not against all legalization; I'm against *dumb* legalization."

1. Do you agree with Kleiman's basic premise to avoid "dumb legalization?" Why or why not?

2. Which of the "policy levers" Kleiman identifies do you think would be most effective against a corporate-dominated marijuana industry?

CHAPTER 2

WHAT THE GOVERNMENT AND POLITICIANS SAY

As a potential multi-billion dollar industry, marijuana has gone mainstream. Proponents for legalization have coalesced into a well-organized and well-funded movement. What's more, they have public opinion on their side: as of this writing, a majority of Americans (58 percent) support legalization.

Consequently, all politicians must now articulate a clear stance on marijuana policy. The challenge facing these politicians is how to stake out ground that capitalizes on public opinion without alienating their more conservative constituents. The Reagan-era "war on drugs" is largely seen as a failure by the media and the public alike. Nonetheless, some outliers on the right still oppose even modest decriminalization efforts. Conversely, left-leaning politicians are pressuring for more comprehensive reform. As of November 2015, Bernie Sanders introduced unprecedented legislation that would reclassify cannabis at the federal level. If passed, marijuana would no longer be a Schedule I controlled substance.

Colorado governor John Hickenlooper is in a unique position to comment on the lessons and aftermath of legalization. In the article below, he notes that his administration opposed legalization, but endeavored to implement the public's will in a careful manner. However, it is important to note that even in states that have passed such legalization, the federal government still considers marijuana use a criminal offense, as we will see in the Office of National Drug Control Policy's "Fact Sheet."

"EXPERIMENTING WITH POT: THE STATE OF COLORADO'S LEGALIZATION OF MARIJUANA," BY JOHN HICKENLOOPER, FROM THE *MILBANK QUARTERLY*, JUNE 3, 2014

On November 6, 2012, voters in Colorado and Washington moved to legalize the use and sale of marijuana by adults 21 and older. The passage of Amendment 64, which amended the Colorado constitution, and Initiative 502, which amended the Revised Code of Washington, marked "an electoral first not only for America but the world." (1) In response to the legalization of recreational marijuana, Colorado is taking a proactive approach. We are working as a convener for all interested parties and experts to shape public policy that utilizes the decades of public health lessons gained from regulating alcohol and tobacco. We have applied these lessons to marijuana and are making every effort in our laws, regulations, and revenue allocations to address public health and safety concerns, prevent young people's use of marijuana, and educate parents and children about the risks of its use.

While Colorado and Washington are the first states to legalize marijuana for recreational purposes, since the 1970s, the national trend has moved toward decriminalization, increased social acceptance, and legalization for medical use. Today, more than half the states in the United States have decriminalized the possession of small amounts of marijuana, approved it for medical use, or legalized it completely. (2) Numerous other states— both liberal and conservative—are considering legalization, indicating that the recreational use of marijuana is no longer a partisan issue. Colorado and Washington are at the forefront of these national trends, and the establishment of rules, regulations, and a policy framework that protects the public's health and safety and prevents underage use will set a baseline for other states' marijuana laws.

Colorado voters passed Amendment 64 with 55% of the vote. Although our administration opposed the legalization of adult-use marijuana, we are committed to fulfilling the will of the voters and directing the responsible regulation of this nascent industry. One of our first steps was to establish a task force to "identify the legal, policy and procedural issues that need[ed] to be resolved, and to offer suggestions and proposals for legislative, regulatory and executive actions that need[ed] to be taken, for the effective and efficient implementation of Amendment 64." (3) This extensive stakeholder process included representatives from all areas affected by marijuana legalization, including health experts, law enforcement, the marijuana industry, the Colorado business community, and marijuana consumers, as well as representatives from state agencies and the Colorado legislature. All groups that might otherwise have had competing and conflicting viewpoints were invited to participate and work together. As a result, we were able to ensure that solutions and recommendations came from an equitable process that gave all interested groups an opportunity to share their positions. In order to guide the work of the task force, all recommendations were required to be based on the following principles:

- Promote the health, safety, and well being of Colorado's youth.
- Be responsive to consumer needs and issues.
- Propose efficient and effective regulation that is clear and reasonable and not unduly burdensome.
- Create sufficient and predictable funding mechanisms to support the regulatory and enforcement scheme.
- Create a balanced regulatory scheme that is complementary, not duplicative, and clearly defined between state and local licensing authorities.
- Establish tools that are clear and practical, so that interactions between law enforcement, consumers, and licensees are predictable and understandable.
- Ensure that our streets, schools, and communities remain safe.
- Develop clear and transparent rules and guidance for certain relationships, such as between employers and

employees, landlords and tenants, and students and educational institutions.

• Take action that is faithful to the text of Amendment 64.

When the federal government updated the guidance for marijuana regulation in August 2013, the US Department of Justice reconfirmed that it would not block any states' laws legalizing marijuana (for recreational or medical purposes) so long as the states established regulations that adequately addressed the following priorities:

• Preventing the distribution of marijuana to minors.
• Preventing revenue from the sale of marijuana from going to criminal enterprises, gangs, and cartels.
• Preventing the diversion of marijuana from states where it is legal under state law in some form to other states. Preventing state-authorized marijuana activity from being used as a cover or pretext for the trafficking of other illegal drugs or other illegal activity.
• Preventing violence and the use of firearms in the cultivation and distribution of marijuana. Preventing drugged driving and the exacerbation of other adverse public health consequences associated with marijuana use.
• Preventing the growing of marijuana on public lands and the attendant public safety and environmental dangers posed by marijuana production on public lands.
• Preventing marijuana possession or use on federal property.

REGULATORY APPROACH

Amendment 64 was pitched to voters as an effort to "regulate marijuana like alcohol," (4) and in many ways we have attempted to do just that, in the retail marijuana center licensing process, the establishment of a nanogram limit for THC in blood to be considered in driving under the influence (DUID), the passage of an excise tax to fund regulatory and preventive programs, and rules concerning public consumption. There also are significant differences, however, in its physical form, its effects on impairment, its production process, and its status in both federal law and international policy. It is these differences that make it necessary to look outside the realm of alcohol regulation to establish commonsense policy.

Given the lack of historic precedent for the legalization of adult-use marijuana, policymakers in Colorado have drawn parallels from other, comparable industries such as gaming and tobacco in addition to alcohol. As businesses seek to maximize profits through the sale of substances that can carry dependence and substance abuse risks, these industries offer useful frameworks, context, research, and promising practices for addressing many of the concerns related to areas like responsible regulation, public health, education, and public safety.

Employing lessons learned from other areas has been significant in the realms of public health and underage use. Drawing on the experience from the Big Tobacco trials of the 1990s, our regulations have placed strict requirements on advertisers, banning outright any ads targeting minors. Looking to the voluntary standards adopted by the alcohol industry, our rules establish that print, television, and radio advertising are not allowed if "more than 30 percent of the audience is reasonably expected to be under the age of 21." (5) We have closely coordinated all public awareness efforts to ensure consistent and effective messaging and have prioritized the distribution of surveillance data and research to promote effective prevention strategies.

PUBLIC HEALTH

Owing to limited funding and study opportunities, marijuana and health professionals and policymakers do not yet know the full scope of the effects of marijuana use; however, the evidence demonstrates that the regular consumption of marijuana does increase the risk of physical and mental health problems. (6) We are working to address these and a wide variety of other public health concerns, with particular emphasis on the developing brain, on which negative impacts are more significant and, in some cases, irreversible. The general consensus among substance abuse professionals is that underage marijuana use can be both dangerous and addictive. Studies show that teenagers' use can lead to negative physical, psychological, and behavioral consequences, such as chronic cough and bronchitis, (7) memory deficits, (8) and a loss of up to 8 points in IQ. (9)

Additional public health issues that we are examining and monitoring as a result of legalization include patterns and prevalence of use, acute health effects from contaminated marijuana products, the safety of edible marijuana products, accidental poisonings of young children from edible products, use among pregnant and breast-feeding women, secondhand smoke, proper marijuana disposal, laboratory testing, substance abuse, potential impaired driving, and occupational health and safety—just to name a few.

We believe that marijuana use has many detrimental effects, and we are not viewing it in a vacuum. We recognize that some people struggle with dependency on multiple substances; as a result, we have an opportunity to proactively direct funding to prevention-focused interventions, which will allow us to avoid costs related to the effects in the long run.

BUDGETING MARIJUANA REVENUES

With revenue starting to come into the state from legal sales, which began on January 1, 2014, we have reinforced, in our proposed budget package, our commitment to the responsible regulation of adult-use marijuana and the effective allocation of resources to protect public health and safety and to prevent underage use. As of February 20, 2014, our budget office is projecting that the state will collect about $134 million in taxes from medical and recreational marijuana sales in fiscal year 2014–2015. (10) Two overall principles guided our recommendations: first, programming should have a direct or indirect relation to marijuana use, and second, we should not create any situations in which state or local governments have an incentive to promote marijuana use. In our proposed budget package we tried to use existing programs in order to minimize duplication, reduce start-up costs, avoid program delays, and build on programs using current research and the best and most promising practices. For many aspects of our proposal, we used a public health prevention framework—public awareness, intervention, treatment, and recovery—to ensure a holistic and responsible use of resources. This budget package represents an important first step toward establishing a broad-based platform, which we can then use to monitor the effects of our policies.

We have worked to strike a balance between creating a level playing field for a new industry and utilizing the most current research to uphold the priority we place on health and safety for all Coloradans. Countless questions have yet to be answered, however. Until the market finds an equilibrium, new policies are given time to settle, and we are able to collect and analyze data about emerging trends as a result of new rules and laws, we cannot presume to guess the net effect of legalizing marijuana use.

With that in mind, we encourage other states considering marijuana legalization not to act rashly or hastily. Legalization is not a panacea for revenue shortfalls. While some areas of government may experience cost reductions, other areas undoubtedly will take on new cost burdens as a result of legalization. At least 8 cabinet-level agencies have serious new responsibilities in this new environment, so states looking in this direction should proceed carefully.

We are attempting to balance myriad issues related to an unprecedented policy change not only for the United States but also for the world. Colorado is a testing ground for this experiment in marijuana legalization, and how well we succeed in accomplishing our objectives will set the stage for other states and countries to examine their own policies regarding marijuana. We believe that we are asking the right questions, attempting to collect the right data, and bringing the right stakeholders to the table. We remain committed to upholding the will of Colorado voters while also creating a robust regulatory environment and focusing on the well-being of all Coloradans.

1. In the years since Colorado has legalized marijuana, which principles (legal, financial, and public health, to take a few examples) are causing the most confusion? Which seem to be running smoothly?

2. What potential dangers of the marijuana industry might be on the horizon?

EXCERPTS FROM "MARIJUANA MYTHS AND FACTS: THE TRUTH BEHIND 10 POPULAR MISPERCEPTIONS," FROM THE OFFICE OF NATIONAL DRUG CONTROL POLICY

INTRODUCTION

Marijuana is the most widely used illicit drug in the United States. According to the National Survey on Drug Use and Health (formerly called the National Household Survey on

Drug Abuse), 95 million Americans age 12 and older have tried "pot" at least once, and three out of every four illicit drug users reported using marijuana within the previous 30 days. (1)

Use of marijuana has adverse health, safety, social, academic, economic, and behavioral consequences. And yet, astonishingly, many people view the drug as "harmless." The widespread perception of marijuana as a benign natural herb seriously detracts from the most basic message our society needs to deliver: It is not OK for anyone—especially young people—to use this or any other illicit drug.

Marijuana became popular among the general youth population in the 1960s. Back then, many people who would become the parents and grandparents of teenage kids today smoked marijuana without significant adverse effects, so now they may see no harm in its use. But most of the marijuana available today is considerably more potent than the "weed" of the Woodstock era, and its users tend to be younger than those of past generations. Since the late 1960s, the average age of marijuana users has dropped from around 19 to just over 17. People are also lighting up at an earlier age. Fewer than half of those using marijuana for the first time in the late 1960s were under 18. By 2001, however, the proportion of under-18 initiates had increased to about two-thirds (67 percent). (2)

Today's young people live in a world vastly different from that of their parents and grandparents. Kids these days, for instance, are bombarded constantly with pro-drug messages in print, on screen, and on CD. They also have easy access to the Internet, which abounds with sites promoting the wonders of marijuana, offering kits for beating drug tests, and, in some cases, advertising pot for sale. Meanwhile, the prevalence of higher potency marijuana, measured by levels of the chemical delta-9-tetra-hydrocannabinol (THC), is increasing. Average THC levels rose from less than 1 percent in the mid-1970s to more than 6 percent in 2002. Sinsemilla potency increased in the past two decades from 6 percent to more than 13 percent, with some samples containing THC levels of up to 33 percent. (3)

Many people who worry about the dangers of heroin or cocaine are less concerned about marijuana, or they consider experimentation with pot an adolescent rite of passage. Such attitudes have given rise to a number of myths in the popular culture. Movies, magazines, and other media commonly show glamorous images and gratuitous use of marijuana, trivializing the risks and ignoring any negative consequences. At the same time, special-interest groups proclaim that smoked marijuana is not only harmless, it's actually good medicine.

Marijuana Myths & Facts looks at 10 popular misperceptions about marijuana and, using the latest research findings and statistical information, explains why they are wrong. The booklet describes the dangers of marijuana and why it is important for society to send a clear, consistent, and credible message to young people about the seriousness of the threat.

MYTH 1: MARIJUANA IS HARMLESS

Marijuana harms in many ways, and kids are the most vulnerable to its damaging effects. Use of the drug can lead to significant health, safety, social, and learning or behavioral problems, especially for young users. Making matters worse is the fact that the marijuana available today is more potent than ever.

Short-term effects of marijuana use include memory loss, distorted perception, trouble with thinking and problem-solving, and anxiety. Students who use marijuana may find it hard to learn, (4) thus jeopardizing their ability to achieve their full potential.

COGNITIVE IMPAIRMENT

That marijuana can cause problems with concentration and thinking has been shown in research funded by the National Institute on Drug Abuse (NIDA), the federal agency that brings the power of science to bear on drug abuse and addiction. A NIDA-funded study at McLean Hospital in Belmont, Massachusetts, is part of the growing body of research documenting cognitive impairment among heavy marijuana users. (5) The study found that college students who used marijuana regularly had impaired skills related to attention, memory, and learning 24 hours after they last used the drug.

Another study, conducted at the University of Iowa College of Medicine, found that people who used marijuana frequently (7 or more times weekly for an extended period) showed deficits in mathematical skills and verbal expression, as well as selective impairments in memory-retrieval processes. (6) These findings clearly have significant implications for young people, since reductions in cognitive function can lead to poor performance in school.

Other impairments observed in frequent marijuana users involve sensory and time perception and coordinated movement, suggesting use of the drug can adversely affect driving and sports performance. (7) Effects such as these may be especially problematic during teens' peak learning years, when their brains are still developing.

MENTAL HEALTH PROBLEMS

Smoking marijuana leads to changes in the brain similar to those caused by cocaine, heroin, and alcohol. (8) All of these drugs disrupt the flow of chemical neurotransmitters, and all have specific receptor sites in the brain that have been linked to feelings of pleasure and, over time, addiction. Cannabinoid receptors are affected by THC, the active ingredient in marijuana, and many of these sites are found in the parts of the brain that influence pleasure, memory, thought, concentration, sensory and time perception, and coordinated movement. (9)

Particularly for young people, marijuana use can lead to increased anxiety, panic attacks, depression, and other mental health problems. One study linked social withdrawal, anxiety, depression, attention problems, and thoughts of suicide in adolescents with past-year marijuana use. (10) Other research shows that kids age 12 to 17 who smoke marijuana weekly are three times more likely than nonusers to have thoughts about committing suicide. (11) A recently published longitudinal study showed that use of cannabis increased the risk of major depression fourfold, and researchers in Sweden found a link between marijuana use and an increased risk of developing schizophrenia. (12)

According to the American Society of Addiction Medicine, addiction and psychiatric disorders often occur together. The latest National Survey on Drug Use and Health reported that adults who use illicit drugs were more than twice as likely to have serious mental illness as adults who did not use an illicit drug. (13)

Researchers conducting a longitudinal study of psychiatric disorders and substance use (including alcohol, marijuana, and other illicit drugs) have suggested several possible links between the two: 1) people may use drugs to feel better and alleviate symptoms of a mental disorder; 2) the use of the drug and the disorder share certain biological, social, or other risk factors; or 3) use of the drug can lead to anxiety, depression, or other disorders. (14)

TRAFFIC SAFETY

Marijuana also harms when it contributes to auto crashes or other incidents that injure or kill, a problem that is especially prevalent among young people. In a study reported by the National Highway Traffic Safety Administration, even a moderate dose of marijuana was shown to impair driving performance. The study measured reaction time and how often drivers checked the rearview mirror, side streets, and the relative speed of other vehicles. (15)

Another study looked at data concerning shock-trauma patients who had been involved in traffic crashes. The researchers found that 15 percent of the trauma patients who were injured while driving a car or motorcycle had been smoking marijuana, and another 17 percent had both THC and alcohol in their blood. (16) Statistics such as these are particularly troubling in light of recent survey results indicating that almost 36 million people age 12 or older drove under the influence of alcohol, marijuana, or another illicit drug in the past year. (17)

LONG-TERM CONSEQUENCES

The consequences of marijuana use can last long after the drug's effects have worn off. Studies show that early use of marijuana is strongly associated with later use of other illicit drugs and with a greater risk of illicit drug dependence or abuse. (18) In fact, an analysis of data from the National Household Survey on Drug Abuse showed that the age of initiation for marijuana use was the most important predictor of later need for drug treatment. (19)

Regular marijuana use has been shown to be associated with other long-term problems, including poor academic performance, (20) poor job performance and increased absences from work, (21) cognitive deficits, (22) and lung damage. (23) Marijuana use is also associated with a number of risky sexual behaviors, including having multiple sex partners, (24) initiating sex at an early age, (25) and failing to use condoms consistently. (26)

MYTH 5: MARIJUANA IS USED TO TREAT CANCER AND OTHER DISEASES.

Under the Comprehensive Drug Abuse Prevention and Control Act of 1970, marijuana was established as a Schedule I controlled substance. In other words, it is a dangerous drug that has no recognized medical value.

Whether marijuana can provide relief for people with certain medical conditions, including cancer, is a subject of intense national debate. It is true that THC, the primary active chemical in marijuana, can be useful for treating some medical problems. Synthetic THC is the main ingredient in Marinol®, an FDA-approved medication used to control nausea in cancer chemotherapy patients and to stimulate appetite in people with AIDS. Marinol, a legal and safe version of medical marijuana, has been available by prescription since 1985.

However, marijuana as a smoked product has never proven to be medically beneficial and, in fact, is much more likely to harm one's health; marijuana smoke is a crude THC delivery system that also sends many harmful substances into the body. In 1999, the Institute of Medicine (IOM) published a review of the available scientific evidence in an effort to assess the potential health benefits of marijuana and its constituent cannabinoids. The review concluded that smoking marijuana is not recommended for any long-term medical use, and a subsequent IOM report declared, "marijuana is not a modern medicine." (42)

Clinical trials of smoked marijuana for therapy are underway through the National Institutes of Health, a major provider of funding for research on the potential medical uses of marijuana. Meanwhile, the best available evidence points to the conclusion that the adverse effects of marijuana smoke on the respiratory system would almost certainly offset any possible benefit.

Some states have removed criminal penalties for possessing marijuana for "medical" use, adding fuel to the debate about using smoked marijuana to reduce suffering. Residents in those states have voted to change the marijuana policy in the mistaken belief that the benefits of smoked marijuana exceed those provided by THC alone. A number of organizations are pushing to make marijuana available for medicinal purposes, (43) but this campaign is regarded by many public-health experts as a veiled effort to legalize the drug.

Moreover, medicines are not approved in this country by popular vote. Before any drugs can be released for public use they must undergo rigorous clinical trials to demonstrate they are both safe and effective, and then be approved by the Food and Drug Administration. Our investment and confidence in medical science will be seriously undermined if we do not defend the proven process by which medicines are brought to market.

MYTH 10: THE GOVERNMENT SENDS OTHERWISE INNOCENT PEOPLE TO PRISON FOR CASUAL MARIJUANA USE

On the contrary, it is extremely rare for anyone, particularly first-time offenders, to get sent to prison just for possessing a small amount of marijuana. In most states, possession of an ounce or less of pot is a misdemeanor offense, and some states have gone so far as to downgrade simple possession of marijuana to a civil offense akin to a traffic violation.

The numbers speak for themselves. In 1997, according to the U.S. Department of Justice's Bureau of Justice Statistics (BJS), only 1.6 percent of the state inmate population had been convicted of a marijuana only crime, including trafficking. An even smaller percentage of state inmates were imprisoned with marijuana *posses-*

sion as the only charge (0.7 percent). And only 0.3 percent of those imprisoned just for marijuana possession were first-time offenders. (72)

More recent estimates from the BJS show that at midyear 2002, approximately 8,400 state prisoners were serving time for possessing marijuana in any amount. Fewer than half of that group, or about 3,600 inmates, were incarcerated on a first offense. (73) In other words, of the more than 1.2 million people doing time in state prisons across America, (74) only a small fraction were first-time offenders sentenced just for marijuana possession. And again, this figure includes possession of *any* amount.

On the federal level, prosecutors focus largely on traffickers, kingpins, and other major drug criminals, so federal marijuana cases often involve hundreds of pounds of the drug. Cases involving smaller amounts are typically handled on the state level. This is part of the reason why hardly anyone ends up in federal prison for simple possession of marijuana. The fact is, of all drug defendants sentenced in federal court for marijuana offenses in 2001, the vast majority were convicted of trafficking. Only 2.3 percent—186 people—were sentenced for simple possession, and of the 174 for whom sentencing information is known, just 63 actually served time behind bars. (75)

It's important to point out that many inmates ultimately sentenced for marijuana possession were initially charged with more serious crimes but were able to negotiate reduced charges or lighter sentences through plea agreements with prosecutors. Therefore, the 2.3 percent figure for simple-possession defendants may give an inflated impression of the true number, since it also includes those inmates who pled down from more serious charges.

The goal of drug laws is not merely to punish, but to reduce drug use and help keep people from harming themselves and others with this destructive behavior. In recent years, with the introduction of drug courts and similar programs, there has been a shift within the U.S. criminal justice system toward providing treatment rather than incarceration for drug users and nonviolent offenders with addiction problems. Today, in fact, the criminal justice system is the largest source of referral to drug treatment programs. (76)

1. In your opinion, is the evidence for the dangers of marijuana use that the government offers convincing? Why or why not?

2. If, as stated, the federal government rarely punishes those who possess small amounts of marijuana, why might it be important to keep these federal possession laws in place?

"RESPONSE TO THE NYT EDITORIAL BOARD'S CALL FOR FEDERAL MARIJUANA LEGALIZATION," BY THE OFFICE OF NATIONAL DRUG CONTROL POLICY STAFF, JULY 18, 2014

SUMMARY: ONDCP RESPONDS TO *THE NEW YORK TIMES* EDITORIAL BOARD'S OPINION THAT THE FEDERAL GOVERNMENT SHOULD LEGALIZE MARIJUANA FOR ADULTS AGED 21 YEARS AND OLDER.

The New York Times editorial board opined in its Sunday July 27, 2014 edition that the Federal government should legalize marijuana for adults aged 21 years and older. *The New York Times* editorial board compares Federal marijuana policy to the failure of alcohol prohibition and advocates for legalization based on the harm inflicted on young African American men who become involved in the criminal justice system as a result of marijuana possession charges. We agree that the criminal justice system is in need of reform and that disproportionality exists throughout the system. However, marijuana legalization is not the silver bullet solution to the issue.

In its argument, *The New York Times* editorial team failed to mention a cascade of public health problems associated with the increased availability of marijuana. While law enforcement will always play an important role in combating violent crime associated with the drug trade, the Obama Administration approaches substance use as a public health issue, not merely a criminal justice problem.

The editorial ignores the science and fails to address public health problems associated with increased marijuana use. Here are the facts:

Marijuana use affects the developing brain. A recent study in *Brain* reveals impairment of the development of structures in some regions of the brain following prolonged marijuana use that began in adolescence or young adulthood. (1) Marijuana use is associated with cognitive impairment, including lower IQ among adult chronic users who began using marijuana at an early age. (2)

Substance use in school age children has a detrimental effect on their academic achievement. Students who earned D's or F's were more likely to be current users of marijuana than those who earned A's (45% vs. 10%). (3)

Marijuana is addictive. Estimates from research suggest that about 9 percent of users become addicted to marijuana. This number increases to about 17 percent among those who start young and to 25–50 percent among people who use marijuana daily. (4)

Drugged driving is a threat to our roadways. Marijuana significantly impairs coordination and reaction time and is the illicit drug most frequently found to be involved in automobile accidents, including fatal ones. (5)

The editors of *The New York Times* may have valid concerns about disproportionality throughout our criminal justice system. But we as policy makers cannot ignore the basic scientific fact that marijuana is addictive and marijuana use has harmful consequences. Increased consumption leads to higher public health and financial costs for society. Addictive substances like alcohol and tobacco, which are legal and taxed, already result in much higher social costs than the revenue they generate.

The cost to society of alcohol alone is estimated to be more than 15 times the revenue gained by its taxation. (6) For this reason, the Obama Administration and the Office of National Drug Control Policy remain committed to drug use prevention, treatment, support for recovery, and innovative criminal justice strategies to break the cycle of drug use and associated crime. This approach is helping improve public health and safety in communities across the United States.

Two recent studies by the nonpartisan RAND Institute suggest that policies making drugs more available would likely not eliminate illicit sales or increase tax revenues to the extent that marijuana legalization advocates predict. The first study examined various methods of measuring marijuana use and found that people under 21 account for a substantial share of marijuana consumption. Under most legalization schemes those under 21 would not be able to purchase marijuana legally; therefore, they would continue to turn to the grey market of illicit or diverted legal marijuana to obtain the drug. The second study examined the likely impact of California's 2012 initiative to legalize marijuana use and concluded that dramatically lowered prices for marijuana as a result of legalization could mean substantially lower potential tax revenue for the state.

We are also keeping a close eye on the states of Washington and Colorado in conformance with the directive provided by the Attorney General in August 2013.

Any discussion on the issue should be guided by science and evidence, not ideology and wishful thinking. The Obama Administration continues to oppose legalization of marijuana and other illegal drugs because it flies in the face of a public health approach to reducing drug use and its consequences. Our approach is founded on the understanding of addiction as a disease that can be successfully prevented and treated, and from which people can recover. We will continue to focus on genuine drug policy reform—a strategy that rejects extremes, and promotes expanded access to treatment, evidence-based prevention efforts, and alternatives to incarceration.

1. The Office of National Drug Control Policy states that debate over marijuana legalization should not just be framed as a "criminal justice problem" but as a "public health issue." Do you think that framing the issue as a matter of public health lends more credence to the federal government's policy on marijuana?

EXCERPTS FROM "SCORECARD OF 2016 PRESIDENTIAL CANDIDATES," BY SMART APPROACHES TO MARIJUANA

Editor's note: The following excerpts are from "score-cards" rating each of the 2016 presidential candidates' positions on marijuana legalization by the anti-legalization Smart Approaches to Marijuana (SAM). Let's see how the candidates stack up.

DEMOCRATIC CANDIDATES

HILLARY CLINTON

HER POSITION

Ms. Clinton does not support legalization of marijuana for recreational use. She has indicated that she would support states and localities "experimenting" with legalization as "laboratories of democracy," but has not specified what that support would entail. She has expressed reservations about "medical" marijuana, but does support overhaul of the criminal justice system to avoid incarcerating low-level drug users, and supports treatment-based approach to addiction issues.

IN HER OWN WORDS

"States are the laboratories of democracy ... I would support states and localities that are experimenting with this." KPPC (July 2014)

"I do support the use of medical marijuana, and I think even there we need to do a lot more research so that we know exactly how we're going to help people for whom medical marijuana provides relief.
"We have got to stop imprisoning people who use marijuana." Democratic presidential debate (October 2015)

GRADE: B-

BERNIE SANDERS

HIS POSITION

Mr. Sanders has stated he would "remove the federal prohibition on marijuana," removing it from the list of controlled substances altogether, although he does not necessarily advocate that states do so. He supports "medical" marijuana programs. While his interest in alternatives to incarceration of drug users is positive, his stance on legalization ironically would undermine his desire to reduce the power of Wall Street.

IN HIS OWN WORDS

"I suspect I would vote yes [on the Nevada initiative to legalize recreational use of marijuana]. And I would vote yes because I am seeing in this country too many lives being destroyed for non-violent offenses. We have a criminal justice system that lets CEOs on Wall Street walk away and yet we are imprisoning or giving jail sentences to young people who are smoking marijuana." Democratic presidential debate (October 2015)

"It's time to tax and regulate marijuana like alcohol." Speech at George Mason University (October 2015)

GRADE: F

REPUBLICAN CANDIDATES

TED CRUZ

HIS POSITION

Mr. Cruz does not support marijuana legalization. He would allow states to legalize, however, a change from his position in 2014.

IN HIS OWN WORDS:

"I actually think [legalization in Colorado] is a great embodiment of what Supreme Court Justice Louis Brandeis called 'the laboratories of democracy.' If the citizens of Colorado decide they want to go down that road, that's their prerogative. I personally don't agree with it, but that's their right." Conservative Political Action Conference (February 2015)

"Now, that may or may not be a good policy, but I would suggest that should concern anyone—it should even concern libertarians who support that policy outcome—because the idea that the president simply says criminal laws that are on the books, we're going to ignore [them]. That is a very dangerous precedent." Interview with Reason (February 2014)

GRADE: B-

MARCO RUBIO

HIS POSITION

Mr. Rubio has shown limited support for "medical" marijuana that does not contain psychoactive compounds, but opposes legalization for recreational use. He would also revisit sentencing and penal law "with great care."

IN HIS OWN WORDS

"[W]e need to enforce our federal laws. Now do states have a right to do what they want? [T]hey don't have a right to write federal policy. ... I don't believe we should be in the business of legalizing additional intoxicants in this country for the primary reason that when you legalize something, what you're sending a message to young people is it can't be that bad, because if it was that bad, it wouldn't be legal." Interview with Hugh Hewitt (April 2015)

GRADE: A

DONALD TRUMP

HIS POSITION

Mr. Trump opposes legalization of marijuana, but would allow states to legalize its use. He supports "medical" marijuana programs. He has not articulated a position on sentencing issues concerning marijuana possession and use.

IN HIS OWN WORDS:

"I think [legalization] is bad, and I feel strongly about that. They've got a lot of problems going on right now in Colorado, some big problems. ...

"[When asked about the states' rights aspect to marijuana laws:] If they vote for it, they vote for it. ...

"I think medical marijuana, 100 percent." Conservative Political Action Conference (February 2015)

GRADE: C+

1. Do these grades seem to split among party lines?

2. Which candidate scores the highest and which candidate scores the lowest according to Smart Approaches to Marijuana?

CHAPTER 3

WHAT THE COURTS SAY

The federal government classifies marijuana as a Schedule I controlled substance. This means that the drug has a high potential for abuse and no proven medical value. It remains a federal crime to use, possess, grow, distribute, or sell any quantity of marijuana for any purpose.

At the state-level, we have a different story. Often lauded as "laboratories of democracy," states are free to experiment with marijuana laws as they see fit. Beginning in 1996, California's Compassionate Care Act made marijuana legal under physician supervision, paving the way for medical marijuana, which is now legal in 23 states. However, what California deemed perfectly legal was a violation of the Controlled Substances Act. In a landmark 2005 case, *Gonzales v. Raich*, the Supreme Court ruled that cannabis use could be federally criminalized even when states approve its use, thus upholding a broad, and to some, problematic, interpretation of congressional power.

As more states legalize cannabis, we can expect many similar lawsuits unless Congress addresses the issue. While the Obama administration pledged not to use Drug Enforcement Administration resources to prosecute marijuana cases in states where marijuana is legal, a future president might do the reverse, and legal precedent is not on the states' side. Reformers such as Bernie Sanders are calling for the immediate descheduling of marijuana on the federal level to end this confusion. But will descheduling marijuana solve the problem?

EXCERPTS FROM *"GONZALES V. RAICH* CASE SUMMARY," BY STREETLAW INC., 2005

GONZALES V. RAICH

ARGUED: NOVEMBER 29, 2004

DECIDED: JUNE 6, 2005

FACTS

The Compassionate Use Act, passed in California in 1996, allowed citizens of the state to use marijuana for medicinal purposes after a doctor has concluded the use would benefit the patient's health. Federal drug law, the Controlled Substances Act, does not provide a similar exemption.

Angel Raich is a citizen of California and has a number of serious health problems, including an inoperable brain tumor, seizures, and chronic pain disorders. For approximately five years, Raich has been using marijuana. According to her physician, she had exhausted "essentially all other legal alternatives." Her medical condition prevents her from growing the marijuana, therefore Raich is dependent on two caregivers to grow it for her.

After a 2002 raid by the federal Drug Enforcement Agency (DEA) of another medical marijuana patient's home, Raich became concerned about being prosecuted for violating federal law. Raich asked the federal district court to prohibit enforcement of federal drug laws against a person in her situation. The district court refused to do this. Raich appealed this decision to the Ninth Circuit Court of Appeals. The Ninth Circuit decided that Raich was entitled to protection from the federal drug laws. That Court said that local, non-commercial cultivation, and sharing, possession, and use of marijuana under the direction of a physician was intrastate (not interstate) commerce. Therefore, it was beyond Congress's power to regulate or prohibit this activity. The federal government appealed this decision to the Supreme Court, and the Supreme Court agreed to hear the case.

ISSUE

Do Federal drug laws (the Controlled Substances Act) exceed Congress's Commerce Clause power when applied to intrastate possession and use of medical marijuana, as authorized by state law?

PRECEDENTS

WICKARD V. FILBURN (1942)

In an effort to increase wheat prices during the Great Depression, Congress passed a law limiting the amount of wheat that some farmers could grow. Farmer Filburn challenged the law, arguing that he intended to use at least some of the wheat for personal consumption, and that Congress could not stop him from growing wheat that he did not intend to sell in interstate commerce. The Supreme Court rejected Filburn's argument and held that Congress can regulate intrastate activity when that activity, in the aggregate, would substantially affect interstate commerce. The farmer's decision to self-supply wheat meant that he would not buy wheat from the market. If many farmers did the same thing, they would substantially affect interstate commerce.

UNITED STATES V. LOPEZ (1995)

Congress passed a law making it a federal crime to carry guns within a school zone. Congress argued that it had the authority to do this under the Commerce Clause because the safety of schools had spillover economic effects on neighboring states that amounted to interstate commerce. The Supreme Court ruled that the law exceeded Congress's Commerce Clause authority because carrying a gun in a school zone is not an *economic* activity. It said that Congress may only regulate:

- Channels of interstate commerce—including highways, waterways, and air traffic.
- People, machines, and things moving in, or used in carrying out interstate commerce.
- Economic activities that have a substantial effect on interstate commerce.

ARGUMENTS FOR RAICH

When medical marijuana patients grow, share, or possess medical marijuana, they are not engaging in economic activity. *U.S. v. Lopez* said that the Commerce Clause did not allow Congress to regulate the non-economic activity in that case.

The patients' activities here are completely intrastate—that is, within the state of California. There is no interstate commerce going on, so regulation is beyond Congress's power under the Commerce Clause.

The federal government argues that there is a national market for marijuana, which makes possession of medical marijuana an economic activity. Simply possessing an item, even if there is a clear market for it, does not mean that you are participating in the market. If you aren't selling or trading the item, you are not participating in the market.

The growth and possession of medical marijuana in this case is policed by the state of California. Californians decided to allow this activity, and the federal government should not interfere.

This situation is not like the wheat-growing activity in *Wickard v. Filburn.* There, the Court discussed the cumulative, or aggregate, effect of many farmers' economic activities. Since the activity in this case is non-economic, there cannot be any cumulative effect on interstate economic markets.

Congress can still regulate illegal drug markets. It just does not have the power to extend that regulation to the non-economic growth, possession, and use of marijuana by medical patients in a state that has legalized such use.

ARGUMENTS FOR GONZALES

Congress, in passing the Controlled Substances Act, was within its power under the Commerce Clause to regulate the national market for drugs which have a high potential for abuse and fostering criminal activity.

The production, distribution, and possession of marijuana can have a substantial effect on interstate commerce, because drugs are often moved and sold between states.

The *Lopez* case dealt with non-economic activity, which is not the case here. Medical marijuana customers still buy, sell, or trade the product, which makes it an economic activity.

In this case, as in *Wickard v. Filburn,* the aggregated effect of allowing the use of marijuana would be staggering. Marijuana produced for medical reasons in California could end up in the illegal national drug market because there is a high demand for illegal drugs across the country.

The government cannot distinguish between marijuana grown for illegal drug purposes and that grown for medical purposes (even if it is lawful within the state). Therefore, all marijuana is subject to the Controlled Substances Act.

It is possible that the marijuana possessed by medical customers in California crossed state lines. In that situation, Congress obviously has the power to regulate it.

DECISION

The Supreme Court ruled in favor of the federal government, 6-3. Justice Stevens wrote the majority opinion and was joined by Justices Kennedy, Souter, Ginsburg, and Breyer. Justice Scalia filed a concurring opinion. Justices O'Connor and Thomas and Chief Justice Rehnquist dissented.

MAJORITY DECISION

The majority decision is based on the Court's previous ruling in *Wickard v. Filburn*. The Court in *Wickard* decided that Congress did have the power, under the Commerce Clause, to regulate an activity even though it was completely intrastate if that activity had a substantial effect on interstate commerce. The Court held that the intrastate production of medical marijuana—like the wheat in *Wickard*—would have a substantial effect on the nationwide supply and demand for the product and therefore it falls squarely within Congress's power to regulate.

The majority also relied on the ruling in *U.S. v. Lopez* in which the Court established that only a "rational basis" was needed for deciding the activity would affect interstate commerce. The Court found that the rational basis in this case is quite easy to identify. Trying to distinguish between locally grown marijuana and non-locally grown would be extremely difficult coupled with the probability of locally grown marijuana ending up in illicit channels was enough to provide a rational basis for Congressional regulation. Furthermore, the Court states that Congress can legislate in this area because prohibiting the use of illegal drugs is an "essential part of the larger regulatory scheme."

Justice Scalia, while agreeing with the outcome, wrote a concurrence in which he stated that the basis for upholding the constitutionality of the Controlled Substances Act (CSA) lies in Congress's power under the Necessary and Proper Clause in combination with the Commerce Clause. Scalia stated that the application of the CSA to purely intrastate activities is essential to the goal of the act—prohibiting marijuana in interstate commerce.

DISSENT

Justice O'Connor wrote a dissent that Chief Justice Rehnquist joined and Justice Thomas joined in part. Justice O'Connor's dissent stressed the foundations of federalism and said that states are seen as laboratories in which they can "try novel social and economic experiments without risk to the rest of the country." As such, California voters had chosen to allow medical marijuana to be available to its citizens. The Court, in upholding the application of the Controlled Substances Act (CSA), destroys this state-based experiment and does so with no evidence of the effect on interstate commerce, only with an assumption of the effect.

Justice Thomas wrote a separate dissent, where he pointed out that by "allowing Congress to regulate intrastate, noncommercial activity under the Commerce Clause would confer on Congress a general police power over the nation." This would, in Thomas's view, provide no meaningful limits on the power of Congress to legislate. The notions of a federal government of limited, enumerated powers would have no meaning.

1. Do you agree with the majority ruling or with the dissent?

2. Which of the arguments for Gonzales do you find most convincing?

EXCERPT FROM "*GONZALES V. RAICH*: IMPLICATIONS FOR PUBLIC HEALTH POLICY," BY SARA ROSENBAUM, FROM *LAW AND THE PUBLIC'S HEALTH*, NOVEMBER–DECEMBER, 2005

On June 6, 2005, the United States Supreme Court decided *Gonzales v. Raich*, (1) a case that addressed the constitutionality of the federal Controlled Substances Act (CSA) as applied to individuals who grow marijuana for personal and medical use under California's Compassion-ate Use Act (CUA). (1, 2) The Court's decision has import-ant implications for the long-standing "federalism" debate under U.S. law, which focuses on the limits of federal power under the Constitution and which has dominated much of the Court's writings in recent years. Because states' power to set public health policy is deeply affected by the course of this debate, (3) this installment of *Law and the Public's Health* is devoted to a discussion of *Gonzales v. Raich* and its implications.

THE CASE

Congress enacted the CSA as Title II of the Comprehen-sive Drug Abuse Prevention and Control Act of 1970. (4) The CSA establishes a rigorous regulatory system relating to the classification, manufacture, distribution, posses-sion, and dispensing of any controlled substance. (5) The Act classifies all controlled substances into five separate schedules based on certain factors: their accepted medi-cal uses, their potential for abuse, and their effects—both physical and psychological. Despite evidence regarding marijuana's potential to relieve pain, both Congress and succeeding Administrations have elected to leave can-nabis subject to a total prohibition under Schedule I of the Act, without provision for legal use. Under the CSA, the manufacture, distribution, or possession of marijuana constitutes a criminal violation. (5)

The state of California, along with "at least nine states," (6) enacted the CUA in response to the health needs of seriously ill individuals. (7) The CUA legalizes the medical use of marijuana by authorizing personal use for medicinal purposes when recommended by a physician. Both Angel Raich and Diane Monson are California residents who used physician-recommended marijuana to manage their conditions. The United States Justice Department under the Clinton Administration took the position that the CSA did not apply to Schedule I drugs such as marijuana in states with medical use laws. However, the Bush Administration adopted a contrary position that, state law notwithstanding, any personal possession of marijuana, even for medical reasons and without any evidence of sale or commercial purposes, amounted to a criminal violation of the CSA. In effect, the Bush Administration eliminated its predecessor's medical use exception. Federal agents then raided Raich's and Monson's homes and seized and destroyed all of Monson's cannabis plants grown for personal use.

Raich and Monson then sued to enjoin enforcement of the CSA, arguing that, as applied to them, the CSA amounted to an unlawful exercise of Congressional power under the Commerce Clause of the United States Constitution, which authorizes Congress to regulate interstate commerce. The plaintiffs' position was that state-sanctioned personal cultivation of physician-recommended medical marijuana amounted to purely *intra*-state, legal, and non-commercial activity and that Congress lacked the power to prohibit such conduct. The plaintiffs lost at trial; however, the United States Court of Appeals for the 9th Circuit enjoined application of the CSA, recognizing state-sanctioned medical marijuana use as a "separate and distinct class of activities" that lay outside the purview of the Act. (8,9) In considering the plaintiffs' Constitutional claims, the Court of Appeals relied on recent Supreme

Court decisions that appeared to bar Congress from reaching purely local conduct. In the first case, *U.S. v. Lopez*, the Court struck down the Guns-Free School Zones Act of 1990, a federal law barring the carrying of guns near schools. (10) In the second case, *U.S. v. Morrison*, the Court invalidated the Violence Against Women Act of 1994, a federal law that made violent acts against women a federal crime. (11)

Writing for a five member Majority, Justice John Paul Stevens, joined by Justices Kennedy, Souter, Ginsberg, and Breyer, reversed the Court of Appeals. (Justice Scalia concurred with the results but on somewhat different grounds.) The Majority (including Justices who typically are considered more "liberal") ruled that, despite the fact that the plaintiffs' conduct was intra-state and involved state-sanctioned medical activities, the Commerce Clause nonetheless vests Congress with the power to reach purely personal and intrastate conduct. Justice Stevens noted, "The question before us, however, is not whether it is wise to enforce the statute in these circumstances; rather, it is whether Congress' power to regulate interstate markets for medicinal substances encompasses the portions of those markets that are supplied with drugs produced and consumed locally." (9)

Indeed, in considering the fundamental Constitutional question raised by the Bush Administration's decision to enforce the CSA in medical marijuana situations, the Majority referred to the considerable evidence supplied over the years, which tended to show that marijuana should not be treated as a Schedule I controlled substance (illegal under all circumstances) but should instead be reclassified as a Schedule II substance (permissible under certain circumstances). In the Majority's view, the scientific wisdom of the law was irrelevant; what mattered was whether the law was minimally rational. In this regard, the Majority pointed out that Congress might have concluded that despite the science, the danger of abuse was so great that cannabis needed to remain a totally prohibited substance. (Again, whether this is a reasonable conclusion is irrelevant for Constitutional law purposes; what matters is whether the law is minimally rational.)

The Majority also concluded that it was irrelevant that the use in this particular case was totally intrastate and involved no commercial trade as such. The Majority pointed to long-standing precedent: a seminal case involving Congress' Commerce Clause powers titled *Wickard v. Filburn.* (12) A World War II–era case involving the power of Congress to impose wage and price controls to prevent inflation, *Wickard* involved the sanctioning of a farmer under the Agricultural Adjustment Act (AAA) for growing excess wheat beyond federally permissible limits for personal consumption. Under the principle of *Wickard*, the Majority argued that Congress could reach even personal and non-commercial intrastate use of a good or product. The proper test of the reaches of Congress' power is not whether the product is meant to move in commerce but whether its production and use has a "substantial economic effect on interstate commerce"; (12) it is the nexus between the conduct and commerce that gives Congress the power to act. The fact that the product in *Wickard* involved a legal commercial commodity was irrelevant in the Majority's view; the only relevant issue was that the proscribed conduct was part of a far broader law aimed squarely at interstate commerce. In essence, the Majority allowed the larger interstate purpose of the Act to swallow up conduct that, considered on its own, might have been unrelated to commerce.

The Majority also distinguished *Lopez* and *Morrison* on the grounds that in neither case was the law aimed at conduct involving commerce. The fatal flaw of both laws according to the Majority was their failure to be grounded in any notion of interstate commerce. Both of the laws, which were declared unconstitutional, were mere "police powers" acts designed to protect public health but without any reference to movement in commerce. The CSA, on the other hand, is aimed squarely at the interstate movement of controlled substances.

Finally, the Majority rejected the notion that the CSA itself did not identify medical marijuana as a separate and distinct activity that lay beyond its reach, since by its very terms, the CSA effectively declared that there could be no acceptable medical use of marijuana. For this reason, the California medical use law was in direct conflict with the terms of the CSA and thus fell under principles of "preemption." No matter how valid a state statute may be under the laws and Constitution of a state, where the law comes into direct conflict with federal law, it is superseded under the Supremacy Clause of the Constitution.

Justice O'Connor, accompanied by Chief Justice Rehnquist and Justice Thomas, filed a strongly worded dissent. In the dissenters view, the Majority decision represented a vast expansion of federal powers to intrude into purely state matters:

> One of federalism's chief virtues ... is that it promotes innovation by allowing for the possibility

that "a single courageous State may, if its citizens choose, serve as a laboratory; and try novel social and economic experiments without risk to the rest of the country." [citation omitted] … This case exemplifies the role of States as laboratories. The States' core police powers have always included authority to define criminal law and to protect the health, safety, and welfare of their citizens…. Exercising those powers, California (by ballot initiative and then by legislative codification) has come to its own conclusion about the difficult and sensitive question of whether marijuana should be available to relieve severe pain and suffering. Today the Court sanctions an application of the federal Controlled Substances Act that extinguishes that experiment, without any proof that the personal cultivation, possession, and use of marijuana for medicinal purposes, if economic activity in the first place, has a substantial effect on interstate commerce and is therefore an appropriate subject of federal regulation. (13)

The dissenters attacked the Majority opinion as a complete departure from the principles of *Lopez* and *Morrison*, arguing that as in both prior cases, the conduct reached in *Raich* involved activities with no nexus to commerce. In Justice O'Connor's view, it was irrelevant that the application of the CSA to personal use for medical purposes came as part of a comprehensive and otherwise legal effort to regulate the movement of controlled substances in commerce; the overall legality of the statute could not save an illegal application of its provisions. The dissent also dismissed the Majority's reliance in *Wickard v. Filburn* on the grounds that the AAA clearly delineated carefully between personal and non-personal use and contained personal use exemptions (none of which applied to the defendant in the case). The reason why the AAA survived its challenge and the CSA should not, according to the dissent, was that unlike the CSA, the AAA clearly tied personal use to commerce and drew specific exceptions.

Justice O'Connor concluded her dissent with the following:

> [T]he Court has endorsed making it a federal crime to grow small amounts of marijuana in one's own home for one's own medicinal use. This over-reaching stifles an express choice by some States, concerned for the lives and liberties of their people, to regulate medical marijuana differently. If I were a California citizen, I would not have voted for the medical marijuana ballot initiative; if I were a California legislator I would not have supported the Compassionate Use Act. But whatever the wisdom of California's experiment with medical marijuana, the federalism principles that have driven our Commerce Clause cases require that room for experiment be protected in this case. (14)

1. Do you see this case as an overreach of the federal government's powers?

2. Is the Supreme Court's ruling logical in your opinion? Why or why not?

"IRRATIONAL BASIS: THE LEGAL STATUS OF MEDICAL MARIJUANA," BY REBECCA DRESSER, FROM THE *HASTINGS CENTER REPORT*, NOVEMBER TO DECEMBER, 2009

In a growing number of states, medical marijuana occupies a dual legal status. The federal Controlled Substances Act (CSA) classifies marijuana as a Schedule I drug, signifying that it has both a high potential for abuse and no acceptable medical use. Patients and physicians are thus subject to the same federal criminal penalties as any other individuals who produce, distribute, or possess marijuana. By mid-2009, however, fourteen states had decided to permit medical marijuana under certain circumstances. Through voter initiatives or legislation, these states have exempted patients and physicians from prosecution for violating state laws governing the use, possession, or cultivation of marijuana.

The disparate legal regimes have generated much litigation, including two cases that reached the U.S. Supreme Court. Both cases rejected challenges to federal enforcement of the CSA in California, the state with the most liberal provisions on medical marijuana. Under the Court decisions, federal authorities could continue to take action against patients, physicians, and others who were protected under state medical marijuana laws.

Two recent legal developments are more favorable to states seeking to permit medical marijuana, however. First, U.S. Attorney General Eric Holder announced that the federal Drug Enforcement Agency would limit future raids and other enforcement activity to individuals violating both federal and state criminal law. This means that people complying with state medical marijuana laws will no longer be targeted by federal law enforcement officials. Holder said that under his leadership, the agency would focus its efforts on large-scale commercial marijuana operations. (1)

In a second development with implications for state marijuana laws, the U.S. Supreme Court declined to review a court decision upholding legislation implementing California's medical marijuana law. In 1996, California voters approved Proposition 215, designed to "ensure that seriously ill Californians have the right to obtain and use marijuana for medical purposes where that medical use is deemed appropriate and has been recommended by a physician." (2) Seven years later, the California legislature enacted the Medical Marijuana Program Act to supplement the earlier law. (3) The 2003 law requires counties to participate in a system that enables patients and caregivers to register and obtain identification cards protecting them from arrest for violating state marijuana prohibitions.

COUNTY VERSUS STATE VERSUS FEDERAL AUTHORITY

California officials unhappy with the state's permissive stance on medical marijuana balked at the mandate to create the identification system. San Diego and San Bernardino counties brought a lawsuit seeking a judicial declaration that they were not required to comply with the state's mandate. According to the plaintiffs, the California law was preempted by the CSA, which fails to exempt medical marijuana from the usual criminal penalties.

The U.S. Constitution gives Congress the power to supersede state law. Over the years, courts have developed principles for determining when federal law preempts state law. Congressional purpose is the central consideration in resolving preemption claims. The easiest case arises when Congress includes in the legislative text an explicit provision on whether the law is intended to preempt state rules. In other cases, courts consider factors such as whether the state law under challenge presents an obstacle to achieving Congress's objectives in enacting the pertinent federal law.

In 2008, a California appellate court ruled against the counties, holding that preemption failed to bar implementation of the California identification card program. (4) As the court noted, the CSA itself states that it is not intended to preempt state laws "unless there is a positive conflict between [the CSA and state law] so that the two cannot consistently stand together." Moreover, the court observed, the states' historical authority over medical practice and state criminal law creates a presumption against federal preemption in these areas.

The California court said that county officials could not use preemption as a basis for rejecting their obligations under the state identification law. According to the court, officials could meet their state law obligations without violating any CSA provision. And the identification law failed to present a significant obstacle to Congress's objective in classifying marijuana as a Schedule I drug because that classification was designed to discourage recreational use, not to control state medical practice. The court conceded that California's broader decision to create a medical use exemption from state marijuana prohibitions "arguably undermines the goals of or is inconsistent with the CSA." But county officials lacked standing to challenge California's general provisions on medical marijuana because those provisions "neither impose obligations on nor inflict direct injury to Counties."

The U.S. Supreme Court's refusal to review the state court decision means that the federal preemption threat has been removed, at least for the time being. And Holder's decision means that people complying with state medical marijuana statutes face no immediate threat of federal prosecution. But the overall legal situation leaves much to be desired, for at least two reasons.

First, neither the state medical marijuana laws nor CSA's marijuana classification rests on solid scientific evidence. Few good studies have evaluated the risks and benefits of smoked marijuana. State medical marijuana laws were passed in reliance on anecdotal and other weak evidence of marijuana's medical benefits. Similarly, the federal judgment that marijuana has no acceptable medical use lacks solid support. The CSA permits marijuana use in research approved by the Food and Drug Administration, but the Drug Enforcement Agency and National Institutes of Health have made it difficult for investigators to obtain the marijuana they need to conduct this research. The agencies have resisted research efforts in the face of reports from groups like the Institute of Medicine and American College of Physicians calling for systematic evaluation of marijuana's risks and potential therapeutic effects. (5) Meanwhile, the FDA has criticized state medical marijuana laws as "inconsistent with efforts to ensure that medications undergo the rigorous scientific scrutiny of the FDA approval process." (6)

MEDICAL VERSUS RECREATIONAL USE

A second problem with the current situation concerns how state and federal officials have responded to the risk that medical marijuana will be diverted to recreational use. California's expansive medical marijuana law permits physicians to recommend marijuana for "any ... illness for which marijuana provides relief." The law also allows individuals to designate as a legally protected "primary caregiver" anyone "who has consistently assumed responsibility for the housing, health, or safety" of the individual.

Journalists report that California's broad approach to decriminalizing medical marijuana has gone a long way toward decriminalizing recreational use, as well. In 2008, the *New Yorker* published a vivid account of how this has happened, featuring physicians who recommend marijuana for problems like anxiety and attention-deficit disorder and marijuana brokers and growers who make a living serving as patients' primary caregivers. (7) Last July, two Associated Press reporters wrote about the broad economic impact medical decriminalization has had in California, producing "chains of for-profit clinics with doctors who specialize in medical marijuana recommendations" and couriers delivering marijuana products for allergies and insomnia "with the practiced efficiency of a home-delivered pizza—and with just about as much legal scrutiny." (8)

In 2008, California's attorney general sought to rein in some of these practices by issuing "Guidelines for the Security and Non-Diversion of Marijuana Grown for Medical Use," but it remains to be seen whether the guidelines will have any real impact. (9) Meanwhile, in the absence of direct debate over whether to decriminalize recreational use of marijuana, communities are grappling with the social and environmental impact of what has become a significant business in California. (10)

Things are no better on the federal side, where officials' concern over potential diversion of medical marijuana seems to account for their lack of cooperation with efforts to study the drug. Many controlled substances approved for medical use can be diverted to illegitimate uses. Indeed, the FDA is attempting to develop better control programs to address widespread and harmful prescription drug abuse. (11) In light of this situation, concern about potential marijuana abuse is an inadequate basis for obstructing research to determine whether marijuana is a safe and effective drug for certain medical conditions.

A better approach would be to treat marijuana as we do other potentially therapeutic agents, subjecting it to rigorous scientific evaluation. State voters and legislators should be more skeptical of claims about marijuana's medical benefits, and federal officials less hostile to efforts to test those claims. If research were to establish that marijuana is a safe and effective intervention for certain conditions, distribution restrictions could be imposed to prevent misuse. Decriminalization of recreational marijuana use should be addressed directly rather than through loose medical marijuana laws like California's. Neither a libertarian nor a "War on Drugs" mentality is a rational basis for the legal status of medical marijuana.

1. Should marijuana laws be decided by specific localities such as counties? Or broadly defined by the federal government? What do you see as the best way to balance preemption claims?

2. Given that many people claim to feel better from the use of marijuana, do you think scientific research is a necessary step to legitimize medical usage? If potentially dangerous and addictive prescription drugs have passed "rigorous scientific testing," can we trust this process?

CHAPTER 4

ADVOCACY GROUPS FOR AND AGAINST LEGALIZATION

There exists a litany of pro- and anti-marijuana legalization advocates, and the Internet provides a free platform for all to air their opinions. As we might expect, not all of these are equally valuable. In selecting the readings below, we have sought statements from influential and established organizations that are capable of articulating their positions in an intelligent and persuasive manner.

On the pro-legalization side, the National Organization for the Reform of Marijuana Laws (NORML) is probably the best known and most established advocacy group. Founded in 1970 by attorney Keith Stroup, NORML has evolved from a tiny niche interest group to a powerful organization employing a large legal team. However, like so many grown-up children of the 1960s, NORML cannot currently be considered radical—a critique of status-quo market capitalism does not figure prominently into their legalization agenda. As we'll see below, NORML supported, albeit tepidly, a controversial ballot-initiative in Ohio that would essentially create an oligarchy of wealthy marijuana producers.

On the other side of the fence, Smart Approaches to Legalization (SAM) believes that legalization will be a net loss for the public, both socially and financially. Although they support decriminalization, they also trivialize the issue by stressing how few people are incarcerated for marijuana. To be sure, those whose lives have needlessly been ruined by a criminal record do not share this opinion.

Public opinion is changing fast on marijuana. Although conclusive data from the states that have legalized recreational marijuana are still scarce, advocacy groups on both sides are eager to spin this complex new reality.

"PRINCIPLES GOVERNING RESPONSIBLE CANNABIS REGULATION," BY THE NORML BOARD OF DIRECTORS, FROM NORML.COM, SEPTEMBER 5, 2015

PRINCIPLES GOVERNING RESPONSIBLE CANNABIS REGULATION

In 1996, a majority of NORML's Board of Directors adopted a set of principles seeking to define "responsible" cannabis use. In recent years, much of the debate surrounding cannabis policy has moved from the question of regulating individual use to how best to regulate the commercial production and retail sale of cannabis. To reflect this ever-evolving political discussion, NORML is issuing an expanded set of principles articulating its positions and sentiments in regard to these more commercial-oriented regulatory efforts.

NORML IS A CONSUMER-ORIENTED LOBBY AND EDUCATIONAL OUTREACH ORGANIZATION, REPRESENTING THE INTERESTS OF ADULTS WHO CHOOSE TO CONSUME CANNABIS IN A RESPONSIBLE** MANNER.

NORML supports legal reforms that permit the responsible use of cannabis by adults. This use includes cannabis consumption for therapeutic, spiritual, and social purposes.

NORML believes that cannabis consumers, like the consumers of other goods, desire a product of high, standardized quality and one that is safe, convenient, and affordable to obtain. Retail cannabis products should be subject to standardized testing by a licensed lab prior to sale to assure that the product is free from harmful pesticides, molds, or other unwanted adulterants, and labeled accurately so the consumer is aware of cannabinoid content. Commercial producers and retail sellers should be licensed and regulated, as are producers/sellers of other commercial goods, and their facilities should be safe and secure.

NORML further supports the establishment and licensing of legal clubs or similar licensed establishments where cannabis consumers can socialize with others in a secure environment outside of their homes.

** Please see NORML's "Principles of Responsible Cannabis Use," reprinted at the end of this article.

NORML DOES NOT OPPOSE THE IMPOSITION OF REASONABLE TAXATION AND REGULATIONS ON THE COMMERCIAL PRODUCTION AND RETAIL SALE OF CANNABIS.

The commercial production and retail sale of recreational cannabis in legal jurisdictions is presently subject to both excise taxes and sales taxes, similar to other commercial goods. The taxation of these goods remains popular with elected officials as well with the general public—particularly among those who do not personally use cannabis, but view the plant's legalization positively as an alternative source of state revenue. The imposition of fair and reasonable taxes on these commercial activities generates support from members of the public who may otherwise show little interest in cannabis law reform.

Such taxation ought not to apply to non-commercial activities involving cannabis. Most importantly, taxation on commercial activities should not be so excessive that it incentivises consumers to obtain cannabis from the black or grey market. In jurisdictions where cannabis is produced and distributed exclusively to qualified patients, such taxes and/or fees ought to be minimal or, ideally, not imposed at all.

Any legal product or commodity that is produced and sold on the retail market will be subject to some level of regulatory oversight. Regulations allow for state and local governments to establish legal parameters for where, when, and how markets operate. Regulations also provide oversight regarding who may legally participate in said markets, and provide guidelines so that those who do so can engage in best practices. Regulations provide clarity to the public, elected officials, as well as to members of law enforcement as to who are the good and bad actors, and provide objective criteria so that one can differentiate between these the two groups.

Virtually all commercial markets are subject to some level of government regulation and the commercial cannabis market will be no different. The role of consumer advocates is to ensure that these regulations are sensible and practical for the individual consumer and that lawmakers do not use the threat of over-regulation to stifle the industry and/or maintain an environment of partial prohibition.

NORML IS NEUTRAL ON POLICIES THAT PROPOSE CAPS LIMITING THE INITIAL NUMBER OF LICENSED CANNABIS PRODUCERS

Several states presently impose caps on the number of licensed cannabis producers and distributors that may legally provide cannabis to either the medical or the retail market. Few states do not impose such caps. These caps vary widely from state to state and market to market, with some states limiting the number of producers to no more than two (Minnesota) or three (Delaware). While NORML believes that a free market promotes both competition and lower prices, both of which inherently are of benefit to the cannabis consumer, NORML's immediate priority is to foster a legal environment where the plant, at least in some specific circumstances, is no longer classified as contraband so that adults who engage in its use responsibly no longer face arrest, incarceration, or a criminal record.

NORML is generally supportive of legislative proposals that meet these immediate criteria. Other regulatory changes in retail production and distribution will likely follow incrementally. NORML believes that advocates are in a better position to leverage for more sensible (and for fewer) regulations in an environment where the adult use of cannabis is codified under the law as opposed to an environment where cannabis is illicit and all users of the plant are criminals.

NORML SUPPORTS THE NEED FOR HOME CULTIVATION

Criminalizing the personal cultivation of cannabis is an arbitrary prohibition that has absolutely no basis in public safety. NORML supports the right of individuals to grow their own cannabis as an alternative to purchasing it from licensed commercial producers. NORML maintains that the inclusion of legislative provisions protecting the non-commercial home cultivation of cannabis serves as leverage to assure the product available at retail outlets is high quality, safe and affordable. That said, as stated previously, NORML's immediate priority is to foster an environment where cannabis is no longer classified as contraband so that adults who engage in its use responsibly no longer face arrest. In general, NORML is supportive of legislative proposals that meet these immediate criteria, even if they do not include, or severely restrict, the ability to cultivate cannabis at home for non-commercial purposes. If and when such measures are enacted restricting personal cultivation rights, NORML believes that lobbying efforts to restore and enact these rights be among advocates' highest priorities.

WHY WOULD NORML SUPPORT LEGISLATIVE EFFORTS OR VOTER INITIATIVES THAT PROVIDE US WITH LESS THAN WHAT WE ULTIMATELY WANT?

Public policy is always evolving. Did those advocating for civil rights halt their efforts following the passage of the federal Civil Rights Act of 1964? Did those advocating for environmental causes cease their efforts after the creation of the US Environmental Protection Agency and/or the Wilderness Act? Did those advocating on behalf of gay/lesbian/transgender issues call it a day after a handful of states legislated in favor of civil unions? No. In each of these cases advocates continued to advocate for further, more expansive changes. And they there were in a stronger position to do so after the passage of these legislative efforts, not prior to them.

Policies that fall short of what advocates desire require continued advocacy in order to achieve future legislative changes. Policies that are enacted in accord with advocates' desires also require further, sustained advocacy to keep those legislative changes in place and to prevent them from being rolled back by political opponents. That is the reality of political advocacy; the job is never "done."

WILL LEGALIZATION UNDERMINE THE NEEDS OF MEDICAL CONSUMERS?

While NORML acknowledges that the medical cannabis market and the recreational cannabis market are not necessarily one in the same, and that individual consumers of these markets may possess needs that differ from one another, we also believe that the advent of a legal cannabis market for all adults will ultimately best serve the needs of those who consume the plant solely for therapeutic purposes. In recent years, medical cannabis only laws have prohibited patients from cultivating their own cannabis, severely restricted patients' access to those with only a handful of qualifying conditions, and limited the type of products dispensed to only non-herbal cannabis formulations and/or specific compounds. These overly restrictive laws are only serving a fraction of the overall patient community that could be assisted by unrestricted adult access to whole-plant cannabis.

"PRINCIPLES OF RESPONSIBLE CANNABIS USE," BY THE NORML BOARD OF DIRECTORS, FROM NORML.COM, FEBRUARY 3, 1996

When cannabis (marijuana) is enjoyed responsibly, subjecting users to harsh criminal and civil penalties provides no public benefit and causes terrible injustices. For reasons of public safety, public health, economics, and justice, the prohibition laws should be repealed to the extent that they criminalize responsible cannabis use. By adoption of this statement, the NORML Board of Directors has attempted to define "responsible cannabis use."

I. ADULTS ONLY

Cannabis consumption is for adults only. It is irresponsible to provide cannabis to children. Many things and activities are suitable for young people, but others absolutely are not. Children do not drive cars, enter into contracts, or marry, and they must not use drugs. As it is unrealistic to demand lifetime abstinence from cars, contracts, and marriage, however, it is unrealistic to expect lifetime abstinence from all intoxicants, including alcohol. Rather, our expectation and hope for young people is that they grow up to be responsible adults. Our obligation to them is to demonstrate what that means. (This provision does not apply to the physician supervised and recommended use of medical cannabis by patients of any age.)

II. NO DRIVING

The responsible cannabis consumer does not operate a motor vehicle or other dangerous machinery while impaired by cannabis, nor (like other responsible citizens) while impaired by any other substance or condition, including some medicines and fatigue.

Although cannabis is said by most experts to be safer than alcohol and many prescription drugs with motorists, responsible cannabis consumers never operate motor vehicles in an impaired condition. Public safety demands not only that impaired drivers be taken off the road, but that objective measures of impairment be developed and used, rather than chemical testing.

III. SET AND SETTING

The responsible cannabis user will carefully consider his/her set and setting, regulating use accordingly. "Set" refers to the consumer's values, attitudes, experience, and personality, and "setting" means the consumer's physical and social circumstances. The responsible cannabis consumer will be vigilant as to conditions—time, place, mood, etc.—and does not hesitate to say "no" when those conditions are not conducive to a safe, pleasant, and/or productive experience.

IV. RESIST ABUSE

Use of cannabis, to the extent that it impairs health, personal development, or achievement, is abuse, to be resisted by responsible cannabis users. Abuse means harm. Some cannabis use is harmful; most is not. That which is harmful should be discouraged; that which is not need not be. Wars have been waged in the name of eradicating "drug abuse," but instead of focusing on abuse, enforcement measures have been diluted by targeting all drug use, whether abusive or not. If cannabis abuse is to be targeted, it is essential that clear standards be developed to identify it.

V. RESPECT RIGHTS OF OTHERS

The responsible cannabis user does not violate the rights of others, observes accepted standards of courtesy and public propriety, and respects the preferences of those who wish to avoid cannabis entirely. No one may violate the rights of others, and no substance use excuses any such violation. Regardless of the legal status of cannabis, responsible users will adhere to emerging tobacco smoking protocols in public and private places.

1. Would you characterize NORML as pro-free market? In light of arguments in favor of non-profit marijuana dispensaries, is this position naïve?

2. Do you believe the majority of the population will adhere to NORML's responsible use guidelines as legalization moves forward? Why or why not?

"LEGALIZATION," BY SAM (SMART APPROACHES TO MARIJUANA), FROM LEARNABOUTSAM.ORG

MARIJUANA USE

Because they are accessible and available, our legal drugs are used far more than our illegal ones. According to recent surveys, alcohol use is used by 52% of Americans and tobacco is used by 27% of Americans. Marijuana is used by 8% of Americans. (1)

When RAND researchers analyzed California's 2010 effort to legalize marijuana, they concluded that the price of the drug could plummet and therefore marijuana consumption could increase. (2)

According to data from the 2012 National Survey of American Attitudes on Substance Abuse, alcohol and cigarettes were the most readily accessible substances for youth 12 to 17 to obtain, with 50% and 44%, respectively, reporting that they could obtain them within a day. Youth were least likely to report that they could get marijuana within a day (31%); 45% report that they would be unable to get marijuana at all. (3)

TAX REVENUE USE

Because marijuana legalization would increase use, any tax revenue gained from legal marijuana would be quickly offset by the social costs. Our examples with legal drugs provide some clarity:

Federal excise taxes collected on alcohol in 2007 totaled around $9 billion; states collected around $5.5 billion. Combined, these amounts are less than 10 percent of the estimated $185 billion in alcohol-related costs to health care, criminal justice, and the workplace in lost productivity. (4)

Tobacco does not yield net revenue when taxed. Each year, Americans spend more than $200 billion on the social costs of smoking, but only about $25 billion is collected in taxes. (5)

Daniel Okrent, whose research into Prohibition inspired Burns's series, wrote last year, "The history of the intimate relationship between drinking and taxing suggests ... that ... [people] indulging a fantasy of income tax relief emerging from a cloud of legalized marijuana smoke should realize that it is likely only a pipe dream." (6)

CRIMINAL JUSTICE SYSTEM

People are not put in prison for small time marijuana use today. Statistics on state-level prisoners reveal that 0.7% of all state inmates were behind bars for marijuana possession only (with many of them pleading down from more serious crimes). (7) Under legalization, more people, not fewer, will be ensnared in the criminal justice system. A fact most people do not know is that alcohol—a legal drug—not cocaine, heroin, or marijuana, is responsible for 2.6 million arrests every year. That is one million more arrests than for all illegal drugs combined. (8)

LEGALIZATION AND THE BLACK MARKET

We also know that the promise of ending violent cartels is far from reality. A recent RAND report showed that Mexican drug trafficking groups only received a minority of their revenue from marijuana. For them, the big money is found in illegal trade such as human trafficking, kidnapping, extortion, piracy, and other illicit drugs. (9) So they are likely to stay around, legal marijuana or not. (10)

EUROPEAN EXPERIENCES

Independent research reveals that in the Netherlands, where marijuana was decriminalized and sold openly at "coffee shops," marijuana use among young adults increased almost 300 percent after a wave of commercialization (15% to 44% lifetime use of young adults; past year use doubled). (11)

There are signs that tolerance for marijuana in the Netherlands is receding. They recently have closed hundreds of coffee shops, and today Dutch citizens have a higher likelihood of being admitted to treatment than nearly all other countries in Europe. (12)

In Portugal, use levels are mixed, and despite reports to the contrary, they have not legalized drugs. In 2001, Portugal started to refer drug users to three-person "panels of social workers" that recommend treatment or another course of action. Use of cocaine did double, but HIV rates slowed and yet drug deaths have been on the rise. These mixed results may or may not have anything to do with the new policy. As the European Monitoring Center's findings concluded: "the country does not show specific developments in its drug situation that would clearly distinguish it from other European countries that have a different policy." (13)

1. Experts against "dumb legalization" have already addressed the taxation shortfall argument—does SAM seem to believe a repeat of the failures of alcohol and tobacco is inevitable? Do you agree?

2. Are comparisons between the United States and the Netherlands or Portugal effective or irrelevant?

CHAPTER 5

WHAT THE MEDIA SAY

Many major newspapers, national magazines, and popular websites are already treating marijuana legalization as a done deal. The legalization of cannabis is a "hot button" issue, which accounts for its heavy representation in the news. Since cannabis reform is supported by more than half of the population (and more than this in liberal markets), writers have some incentive to appear on the same side of the issue as their readers. Moreover, legalization mobilizes enduring American values such as personal freedom and the belief in a free market system. Despite these reasons for media support, many people, such as David Frum of *Commentary*, still oppose the idea.

The media is also responsible for trumpeting marijuana's new public image. No longer the province of hippies and degenerates, the pot industry is now attracting an emerging professional class, as we'll see in the profile of lobbyists working with the National Cannabis Industry Association.

Lastly, a critical review of former drug czar William Bennett's staunchly prohibitionist new book and another look at Issue 3, the recently defeated Ohio ballot initiative, as reported by a local paper, round out our media chapter.

"DON'T GO TO POT: THE CASE AGAINST THE LEGALIZATION OF MARIJUANA," BY DAVID FRUM, FROM *COMMENTARY*, APRIL 1, 2014

The 50 states are sometimes called "laboratories of democracy." Although the expression is intended to high-light in flattering terms how innovative they can be, it also suggests that the states' political experiments can and do fail. In the event of failure, the hope must be that damage can be stopped at the state line. Today, the experiment of state-by-state marijuana legalization is failing before our eyes—and failing most signally where the experiment has been tried most boldly. The failure is accelerating even as the forces pushing legalization are on what appears to be an inexorable march of marijuana.

In November 2012, the states of Colorado and Washington voted to legalize the sale of marijuana to any adult consumer. Advocates of legalization carried the vote with a substantial campaign budget, a few million dollars, and a brilliant slogan: "Drug dealers don't ask for

ID." The implied promise: Marijuana legalization would be joined to tough enforcement to keep marijuana away from minors. After all, persistent and heavy marijuana use among adolescents has been shown to reduce their IQ as adults by 6 to 8 points. An Australian study of identical twins found that a twin who started using cannabis before age 17 was 3 times more likely to attempt suicide than the twin who did not. People in Colorado had good reason to worry about teen drug use. Colorado voters had approved a limited experiment with medical marijuana in 2000. A complex series of judicial and administrative decisions in the mid-2000s overthrew most restrictions on the dispensing of marijuana. Between 2009 and 2012, the number of dispensaries jumped past 500, and the number of medical cardholders multiplied from roughly 1,000 to more than 108,000.

With so many medical-marijuana card-holders walking about, it was simply inevitable that some would resell their marijuana to underage users. A 2013 study of Colorado teens in drug treatment found that 74 percent had shared somebody else's medical marijuana. The number of occasions on which they had shared averaged over 50 times. According to a report by the Rocky Mountain High-Intensity Drug Trafficking Area, Colorado teens, by 2012, were 50 percent more likely to use marijuana than their peers in the rest of the country.

Debates about marijuana tend to travel pretty fast into the domain of libertarian ideology: *I'm a consenting adult, why can't I do what I want?* Yet the best customers for the marijuana industry are not adults at all. The majority of people who try marijuana quit by age 30. Adults in their twenties are significantly less likely than high school students to smoke; 14 percent of twenty-somethings say they smoke marijuana, while 22.7 percent of 12th-graders smoke at least once a month, and 6.5 percent say they smoke every day.

Why do people quit using marijuana as they mature? Your guess is as good as anybody else's, but whatever the reason, the trend presents marijuana sellers with a marketing problem. Yet there is promising news from the emerging marijuana industry's point of view: People who start smoking in their teens are significantly more likely to become dependent than people who start smoking later: about 1 in 6, as opposed to 1 in 10. Start them young; keep them longer. Very rationally, then, the marijuana industry is rolling out products designed to appeal to the youngest consumers: cannabis-infused soda, cannabis-infused chocolate taffy, cannabis-infused jujubes.

The promise that legalization will actually protect teenagers from marijuana is false. So, too, are the other promises of the legalizers. It is false to claim that marijuana legalization will break drug cartels. Those cartels will continue to traffic in harder and more lucrative drugs, such as heroin, cocaine, and methamphetamine. Criminal cartels may well stay in the marijuana business, too, marketing directly to underage users. Public policy is about trade-offs, and marijuana users need to face up to the trade-off they are urging on American society. Legal marijuana use means more marijuana use, and more marijuana use means above all more teen marijuana use.

Proponents of marijuana legalization often question why the law bans marijuana but not alcohol or tobacco. One important difference is that alcohol and tobacco are drugs on the decline. Since 1980, per capita consumption of alcohol has dropped almost 20 percent. One-third of Americans smoked tobacco in 1980; fewer than one-fifth smoke today. The progress against drunk driving is even more remarkable: Fatalities caused by drunk drivers have decreased by more than half since 1982.

The reduction in tobacco and alcohol use has been hastened by increasingly restrictive laws that govern where and how these products may be consumed. Tobacco-smoking has been banned on planes, in restaurants, and in almost all public places. The drinking age, reduced in the 1970s from 21 to 18 in most states, was restored to 21 by federal action in the 1980s. Tobacco taxes have been steeply hiked. Bars that served intoxicated patrons face rising tort risk.

With marijuana, however, the law is heading in the opposite direction, and has been for some time. Since 1996, 20 states and the District of Columbia have approved "medical marijuana" laws, whereby people who obtain a prescription from a doctor can legally use or purchase marijuana. As in Colorado, many of these supposed medical regimes are degenerating into legalization by another name. Oregon, for example: At the end of 2012, it was home to 56,531 medical-marijuana patients. The majority of these 56,000-plus permissions were approved by only nine doctors. One doctor—an 80-year-old retired heart surgeon in Yakima—approved 4,180 medical-marijuana applications in a span of 12 months. Only 4 percent of Oregon's medical-marijuana patients, as of the end of 2012, suffered from cancer. Only 1 percent were diagnosed with HIV/AIDS. The large majority, 57 percent, cited unspecified "pain" as the ailment for which treatment was sought. Yet none of the nine doctors who wrote the majority of the marijuana prescriptions was a pain specialist.

Fewer than 2 percent of California card holders have HIV, glaucoma, multiple sclerosis, or cancer: One survey found that the typical California medical-marijuana patient was a healthy 32-year-old man with a history of drug and alcohol abuse. Here, too, some doctors are signing thousands of recommendations after only the scantiest examination—or none at all. An NBC news investigator in Los Angeles visited one dispensary, was examined by a man who later proved to be an acupuncturist and massage therapist, and then received a prescription signed by a doctor who lived 67 miles away.

In the words of Los Angeles police chief Charlie Beck, most dispensaries are "for-profit businesses engaged in the sale of recreational marijuana to healthy young adults." By early 2012, Los Angeles contained almost eight times as many dispensaries as Starbucks coffee shops. The city became alarmed that the customers who congregated at these dispensaries were active in crimes from robbery to murder. By July, the City Council voted unanimously to shut down all of the nearly 800 known dispensaries in the city. The marijuana lobby succeeded in preventing that ban from going into effect, so the next year, the city government tried a different approach: a local referendum called Proposition D to cap the number of dispensaries at 135, raise taxes on marijuana sales, and forbid dispensaries to locate near primary, middle, and high schools.

The proposition was approved, but this approach also proved ineffective. In the words of *Medical Marijuana Business Daily* (yes, it exists):

Officials have actually only forced about 70 dispensaries to close so far. While some other dispensaries shut down on their own to avoid legal troubles, most did not. That means at least 700—possibly more—illegal shops are still open.

"What happened is that we're really trying to put a Band-Aid on some crazy open wound, and it's not big enough to stop the bleeding," said Adam Bierman, who runs the consultancy MedMen. "Prop D as a concept is half decent, but there's really no way to enforce it."

Marijuana does possess certain medicinal properties. So does opium. But we don't allow unscrupulous quacks to write raw opium prescriptions for anyone willing to pay $65. And if we did, would anybody be surprised that the vast majority of opium buyers were not recovering from surgery—and that many of them shared or resold some of their opium to underage users?

Some older adults have a hard time crediting the dangers of marijuana use because they imagine the marijuana on sale today is the same low-grade stuff they smoked in college. The marijuana sold in the 1980s averaged between 3 and 4 percent THC, the psychoactive ingredient. Today's selectively bred marijuana averages over 12 percent THC, with some strains reaching 30 percent. Hundreds of YouTube videos will show you how to combust a marijuana wax with butane, to boost the THC content to 90 percent. As marijuana consumers shift from smoking to ingesting marijuana, they can ingest larger and larger doses of THC at a time. Since 2006, Colorado emergency rooms have seen a steep rise in the number of patients arriving panicked and disoriented from excess THC, including a near doubling of patients ages 13 and 14.

It's said that nobody ever died from a marijuana overdose. Nobody ever died from a tobacco overdose either, but that doesn't prove tobacco safe. Of all the dangers connected to marijuana, the most lethal is the risk of automobile accident. Marijuana-related fatal car crashes have nearly tripled across the United States in the past decade. Marijuana legalizers may counter: Can't we just extend laws against drunk driving to stoned driving?

Unfortunately, it's not so easy. What exactly defines marijuana impairment remains fiercely contested by an increasingly assertive marijuana industry. It took Colorado four tries to enact a legal definition of marijuana impairment: five nanograms of THC per milliliter of blood. Yet even once enacted, the standard remains very difficult to enforce. Alcohol impairment can be detected with a Breathalyzer. Marijuana impairment is revealed only by a blood test, and long-established law requires police to obtain a search warrant before a blood test is administered.

More important than catching impaired drivers after the fact is deterring them before they get behind the wheel. In the absence of a blood-testing kit, marijuana users themselves will find it difficult to know how much is too much. *Time* recently quoted a spokes person for the Colorado Department of Transportation: "It's not like alcohol. People metabolize it differently. There are different potencies," the official said. "So there's really no solution in terms of saying "you're now at the limit.' I just don't think there's enough research that we can say, 'Wait x amount of hours before getting on the road.' I don't know whether it's five hours or 10 hours or the next day. We just don't know."

Back in 2007, a survey by the National Highway Traffic Safety Administration found that on any given Saturday night, about 12 percent of drivers tested positive for alcohol; about 6 percent for marijuana. Since then, 10 more states and the District of Columbia have adopted medical-marijuana regimes, which surely means even more buzzed drivers on the roads.

Yet the most pervasive harm of marijuana may be psychic rather than physical. A battery of studies have found regular marijuana use to be associated with worse outcomes at school, social life, and work. I use the cautious phrase "associated with," because it's far from clear whether marijuana use is a cause or an effect of other problems—or (most likely) both cause and effect. An isolated, underachieving kid starts smoking marijuana. That kid then descends deeper into isolation and under-achievement. Marijuana may not have been the "cause" of the kid's malaise, but it intensifies the malaise and may inhibit or even prevent his emergence from it.

The negative spiral of despondency leading to marijuana use, leading to deeper and more protracted despondency, makes the present moment a particularly unpropitious one for marijuana legalization. The United States is currently recovering feebly from the gravest economic crisis since the Great Depression. Prospects for young people especially have narrowed. Are we really going to say to them: "Look, we haven't got jobs for you, your chances at marriage are dwindling, you may be 30 before you can move out of your parents' place into a home of your own, but we'll make it up to you with pot, video games, and online porn"? They want to start life, but they are being offered instead only narcotic dreams.

As human beings, our judgment is not only imperfect, but is prone to fail in highly predictable ways. Insert a recurring charge onto our phone bill, and we will soon cease to notice it. We evolved under conditions where sugars and salt were scarce, and so we will eat far more than we need if given the chance. We overestimate our luck and will gamble our money in ways that make no mathematical sense. Our brains are wired for addictions. If a substance can trigger that addiction, it can overthrow all the reasoning and moral faculties of the mind.

Lucrative industries have arisen to exploit these weaknesses in ways highly harmful to their customers. And the bold irony is that when their practices are challenged, they'll invoke the very principles of individual choice and self-mastery that their industry is based on negating and defeating. So it was with tobacco. So it is with casino gambling. So it will be with marijuana.

Proponents of marijuana legalization do make a valid point when they worry that marijuana laws are enforced too punitively—and that this too punitive approach inflicts disparate punishment on minority users as compared with white users. Ordinary marijuana users should receive civil penalties; repeat users belong in treatment, not prison; communities should experience law enforcement as an ally and supporter of local norms, not an outside force stamping young people with indelible criminal records for mistakes that carry fewer consequences for the more affluent and the better connected. It's also true, however, that these alternative methods can succeed only if the background rule is that marijuana is illegal. It's very often the threat of criminal sanction that impels users to seek the treatment they need, while still young enough to turn their lives around.

The illegal U.S. market for marijuana is already twice as big as the market for coffee. As that market is legalized, it will expand, and the industry that serves the market will be emboldened to hire lobbyists to promote its continued expansion. The vision offered by some academics of a legal but noncommercial marijuana market shows little realism about American government. American legislatures exhibit notoriously poor resistance against checkbook-wielding special interests.

The resistance will be all the weaker since the costs of marijuana legalization will be borne by people to whom American legislatures pay scant attention anyway. Marijuana retailers will be located most densely in America's poorest neighborhoods, just as liquor and cigarette retailing is now. Out of whose pockets will the marijuana taxes of the future be paid? Whose addiction and recovery services will be least well funded? In a society in which it is already sufficiently difficult for people to rise from the bottom, who'll find that their rise has become harder still?

1. How does the author support the claim that legalizing marijuana will hurt those at the bottom of society most? Is this argument convincing?

2. Which potential benefits of legalization does the author believe have merit? Which benefits does he choose to ignore?

"A DAY IN THE LIFE OF A MARIJUANA LOBBYIST," BY CHRIS MOODY, FROM *YAHOO NEWS*, MARCH 17, 2014

In the center of the crowded basement cafeteria of the Rayburn House Office Building on Capitol Hill, Big Pot's mobile war room was humming.

While hundreds of congressional staffers lunched around them, a group of foot soldiers in the effort to legalize marijuana stood over a rectangular table cluttered with plates of sushi and documents, busily stuffing white folders with literature about the need for the federal government to change the nation's cannabis laws. Each folder, which would be delivered to a congressional office on one of the floors above, needed a primer on bills that had been introduced to reform banking and tax laws for the cannabis industry, a letter urging co-sponsorship of the bills, a position paper from Grover Norquist's Americans for Tax Reform, and a *New York Times* story about the burgeoning marijuana industry.

It was the final hours of a two-day Washington, D.C., blitz by the National Cannabis Industry Association, the 3-year-old lobbying arm of the country's increasingly organized legal marijuana industry. With just a few hours remaining until the advocates' scheduled flights home, there were still several offices to visit.

On a laptop at the table, NCIA events manager Brooke Gilbert scanned and updated a detailed Google spreadsheet that listed all the association members who had flown to the capital to help with the group's annual lobby day, ticking off the names of offices on Capitol Hill they had visited and those they still needed to stop by.

Other members of the association—a mixture of pot growers, marijuana dispensary owners, scientists, doctors and activists from around the country—sat at nearby tables and talked excitedly about their own meetings with lawmakers and congressional staffers. By day's end, the members would hold meetings with more than 60 offices about pot and the legal, new, booming industry of growing and selling the psychoactive plant.

The advocates have had great success at the state level. Already 20 states and the District of Columbia allow legal medical marijuana, and Washington and Colorado last year became the first states to make pot legal for recreational use. But changes in federal laws have lagged. That's one reason that, at the end of 2010, marijuana-related business owners pooled their resources to form the NCIA.

Now the cannabis industry is solidifying its presence in the halls of Congress. Late last year, the NCIA hired Michael Correia, a former Republican congressional staffer, to lobby for the industry full time in Washington, D.C. Previously, he worked as a field representative for Tennesee Republican Rep. Diane Black and spent two years as the director of federal affairs for the conservative American Legislative Exchange Council.

The group relies on survey data from pollster Celinda Lake to update its arguments and provide data on the state of play. A 22-member board and a staff of five direct operations from the group's headquarters in Denver, Colo. The group represents more than 400 companies in 20 states that together bring in more than $2 billion in revenue annually.

If there was one feature that stood out most about the marijuana activists last week, it was that they did not stand out at all. With the exception, perhaps, of one woman dressed in a tailored pantsuit and wearing natural red dreadlocks that stretched to her waist, the cannabis industry team was indistinguishable from the routine mix of lobbyists, staffers, advocates and journalists in the Rayburn halls.

That's intentional: The pot lobby is desperately seeking legitimacy—and taking the steps to achieve it.

"We're respectable, responsible businesspeople," said Dorian Deslauriers, an NCIA member who runs a lab in Massachusetts that tests and analyzes medical marijuana. "We are just like the rest of the industries in America."

While the association doesn't own an imposing building on Capitol Hill or K Street that bears its name— Correia works from a small office in downtown D.C.— the NCIA's lobbying tactics mirror those of other industries. For weeks before the group's members arrived in Washington, Correia set up meetings with legislative offices. Over two days, supporters of the cannabis cause targeted lawmakers on the Banking, Finance, and Judicial committees in both chambers of Congress, and met with lawmakers who represent states with NCIA members. Most of the meetings lasted about a half-hour, attendees said, and focused on two main priorities: legislation permitting cannabis industry organizations to write off business expenses on their taxes and a measure to allow federally insured banks to work with the businesses, even though they're engaging in activity that's still considered illegal under federal law.

Where they could, NCIA staffers let the business owners do the talking.

"We're not expecting, or even wanting, our members to go in with some perfectly polished presentation. It's not the point," said Taylor West, NCIA's deputy director. "We have the lobbyist who will be there when we leave who can follow up with technical questions. What we want is to communicate that these are very real struggles that responsible business owners are dealing with."

As far as federal law is concerned, much of what these companies do remains illegal. The Drug Enforcement Administration still labels their main product a "Schedule 1" drug along with heroin and LSD. While the businesses that NCIA represents function legally within the states where they are based, they are at constant risk of federal prosecution, should the Department of Justice decide to strictly enforce the law.

Because of this, businesses in the industry can't write off their expenses for federal tax purposes, a benefit offered to all companies, including the legal brothels in Nevada. And banks are hesitant to lend to or allow accounts for these companies, leading some to store massive amounts of cash and place themselves at higher risk for theft.

For now, fixing these issues—not national legalization—is the advocates' top priority.

"It's important that we're treated like any other business," said Ean Seeb, a member of the NCIA board. "That's the consistent message: Treat us like any other business."

Converting congressmen to this way of thinking is slow-going. While there are a handful of lawmakers on both sides of the aisle who actively support the cannabis industry, particularly Democratic Reps. Earl Blumenauer of Oregon and Jared Polis of Colorado and California Republican Rep. Dana Rohrabacher, many members of Congress are fearful of touching the issue. Most have opposed efforts to decriminalize marijuana for their entire careers and are unlikely to changes their positions quickly.

But compared to how lawmakers treated industry activists even just a few years ago, recent congressional interest in talking to legalization advocates is stunning.

"We've seen a lot more interest this year and, anecdotally at least, we're seeing more legit senior staff that we're talking to," West said. "Legislative affairs people, not constituent services people."

Said Seeb after a series of meetings on Thursday: "They're finally taking it seriously. They're asking the right questions."

Of course, that's not a universal position, he added: "At the same time, there are people completely dismissing us."

As part of the NCIA lobbying effort, Correia also organized a public briefing in the House Budget Committee room on Capitol Hill, open to anyone interested in the issue. The event included brief speeches from sympathetic members of Congress, a presentation about polling data on changing attitudes toward marijuana and stories from business owners in the industry.

Of all the speakers present, it was the lawmakers, many of whom have worked on the issue for decades without much progress, who appeared the most passionate.

"We keep needing bigger and bigger rooms," an ecstatic Blumenauer said when he looked over the group of about 80 at the briefing. "Isn't that wonderful?!"

While movement on the issue has seemed staggeringly slow—Blumenauer said he cast his first vote to decriminalize marijuana in the Oregon Legislature in the early 1970s—the rapid change in public views during just the past few years has almost caught the pro-legalization lawmakers off-guard. A CNN-Opinion Research poll in January found that 55 percent of Americans believe marijuana should be legalized, a statistic that jumped by 12 percentage points from just a year before.

States around the country are preparing for votes to legalize the drug later this year, opening the possibility for billions more in revenue for those in the industry.

"The public is shifting very, very dramatically," Lake, the pollster, said, citing a trove of statistics about attitudes toward marijuana. "This is an issue that's absolutely at its tipping point."

The good news for pot advocates, she said, was that although many in the U.S. still oppose legalization, they won't take to the streets against it. Unlike hot-button issues like abortion or same-sex marriage, those who oppose marijuana legalization don't come out to vote just because it's on the ballot.

"People don't mobilize or turn out against marijuana," she said. "They shrug their shoulders, they wish their grandkids didn't use it, but they don't vote to beat marijuana."

Washington, however, has been slow to catch up. With nearly $2 billion flowing legally through the economy now that several states have legalized the plant's production and use, the federal government still hasn't decided how to address it. President Barack Obama's Department of Justice has said it won't prosecute businesses in the industry that operate under state law and is allowing banks to do business with them, but pot industry activists say they need Congress to move in order to give banks and business owners further security that their investments will be protected.

"We're in this Never Never Land on Capitol Hill. The administration and Congress is in denial, and we're the problem," Blumenauer said. "We're trying to get the administration to get real."

Accomplishing this, of course, will require support from members of both political parties.

On the right, Republicans have just recently begun to nibble at the edges of reform. Conservatives such as Sens. Rand Paul of Kentucky, Mike Lee of Utah and John Cornyn of Texas have promoted an effort to re-examine sentencing laws for nonviolent drug criminals. Republican governors such as Rick Perry of Texas and Bobby Jindal of Louisiana have also moved forward in their own states to reduce mandatory minimum sentences for drug users.

Fear is one of the main drivers moving against widespread legalization, said Rohrabacher, the California Republican.

"If it were a secret ballot, a majority of my Republican friends would vote for [legalization]," Rohrabacher said. "They're afraid that if they step up to the plate, their next election, they will be portrayed by their opponent as 'The Friend of the Drug Cartel.'"

The task and challenge, marijuana advocates say, is providing lawmakers "evolving" on the issue with the data and information that will help them explain why they've flipped. As with any shift in position, that takes time. After years of opposing legalization, it's difficult for any public figure to suddenly change course.

But the representatives of Big Pot see time, public opinion, and data on their side.

"Polling is through the roof," West said. "The elected just have to catch up."

1. What do you think about the increasing activity of pro-marijuana lobbying groups such as those affiliated with the NCIA? Is this evidence for the reality of "big tobacco 2.0"?

"BILL BENNETT'S POT PREVARICATIONS: A FORMER DRUG CZAR'S DAZED AND CONFUSED DEFENSE OF MARIJUANA PROHIBITION," BY JACOB SULLUM, FROM *REASON*, MAY 2015

Going to Pot: Why the Rush to Legalize Marijuana Is Harming America, by William J. Bennett and Robert A. White, Center Street, 240 pages, $26

"With marijuana," declare William J. Bennett and Robert A. White in *Going to Pot*, their new prohibitionist screed, "we have inexplicably suspended all the normal rules of reasoning and knowledge." You can't say they didn't warn us.

The challenge for Bennett, a former drug czar and secretary of education who makes his living nowadays as a conservative pundit and talk radio host, and White, a New Jersey lawyer, is that most Americans support marijuana legalization, having discovered through direct and indirect experience that cannabis is not the menace portrayed in decades of anti-pot propaganda. To make the familiar seem threatening again, Bennett and White argue that marijuana is both more dangerous than it used to be, because it is more potent, and more dangerous than we used to think, because recent research has revealed "long-lasting and permanent serious health effects." The result is a rambling, repetitive, self-contradicting hodgepodge of scare stories, misleading comparisons, unsupportable generalizations, and decontextualized research results.

Bennett and White exaggerate the increase in marijuana's potency, comparing THC levels in today's strongest strains with those in barely psychoactive samples from the 1970s that were not much stronger than ditch weed. "That is a growth of a psychoactive ingredient from 3 to 4 percent a few decades ago to close to 40 percent," they write, taking the most extreme outliers from both ends. Still, there is no question that average THC levels have increased substantially as Americans have gotten better at growing marijuana. Consumers generally view that as an improvement, and it arguably makes pot smoking safer, since users can achieve the same effect while inhaling less smoke.

But from Bennett and White's perspective, better pot is unambiguously worse. "You cannot consider it the same substance when you look at the dramatic increase in potency," they write. "It is like comparing a twelve-ounce glass of beer with a twelve-ounce glass of 80 proof vodka; both contain alcohol, but they have vastly different effects on the body when consumed." How many people do you know who treat 12 ounces of vodka as equivalent to 12 ounces of beer? Drinkers tend to consume less of stronger products, and the same is true of pot smokers—a crucial point that Bennett and White never consider.

When it comes to assessing the evidence concerning marijuana's hazards, Bennett and White's approach is not exactly rigorous. They criticize evidence of marijuana's benefits as merely "anecdotal" yet intersperse their text with personal testimonials about its harms ("My son is now 27 years old and a hopeless heroin addict living on the streets ..."). They do Google searches on "marijuana" paired with various possible dangers, then present the alarming (and generally misleading) headlines that pop up as if they conclusively verify those risks. They cite any study that reflects negatively on marijuana (often repeatedly) as if it were the final word on the subject. Occasionally they acknowledge that the studies they favor have been criticized on methodological grounds or that other studies have generated different results. But they argue that even the possibility of bad outcomes such as IQ loss, psychosis, or addiction to other drugs is enough to oppose legalization.

"Let us hypothesize severe skepticism and say, for argument's sake, all these studies have a 5 percent chance of being right," Bennett and White write. Even then, they say, the continued prohibition of marijuana would be justified, noting that the painkiller Vioxx was pulled from the market in 2004 "when it was discovered 3.5 percent of its users suffered heart attacks as opposed to 1.9 percent [of those] taking a placebo." Bennett and

White thus conflate a 5 percent chance that a drug poses any danger at all with a 5 percent chance that a given user will suffer serious harm. They are not the same thing. Bennett and White also imply that if "all these studies have a 5 percent chance of being right," that is equivalent to something like an 84 percent increase in risk (as seen with Vioxx). That is not right either.

Just as puzzling, Bennett and White put a lot of effort into arguing, quite unconvincingly, that "marijuana is at least as harmful as tobacco and alcohol," even though they repeatedly say it does not matter whether that's true. "More than smoking tobacco or drinking alcohol, smoking marijuana can damage the heart, lungs, and brain," they write. "It is simply untrue that tobacco is more harmful than marijuana."

They never substantiate these claims, because they can't. As measured by acute toxicity, impact on driving ability, frequency of addiction, and the long-term effects of heavy consumption, alcohol is clearly more dangerous than marijuana. That point has been acknowledged not only by President Barack Obama but by his drug czar and even by Patrick Kennedy, co-founder of the anti-pot group Project SAM. The difference in risk is also recognized by a large majority of Americans, making Bennett and White's attempt to deny it even more quixotic.

The argument that marijuana is just as deadly as tobacco is equally bizarre, relying on the findings of a few scattered studies without regard to their strength or reproducibility. Bennett and White say, for example, that marijuana, like tobacco, causes lung cancer and cardio-vascular disease. But according to a review published by the Colorado Department of Public Health and Environment (CDPHE) in January, there is "mixed evidence for whether or not marijuana smoking is associated with lung cancer." The CDPHE explains that "mixed evidence ... indicates both supporting and opposing scientific findings for the outcome with neither direction dominating." The same report says there is only "limited evidence that marijuana use may increase risk for both heart attack and some forms of stroke." By "limited evidence," the CDPHE means there are "modest scientific findings that support the outcome, but these findings have significant limitations."

In other words, the hazards that Bennett and White cite, unlike the hazards of cigarette smoking, are unproven. Even if they were well established, there is no reason to think their magnitude would be similar, given the huge difference between the doses of toxins and carcinogens absorbed by a typical tobacco smoker and the doses absorbed by a typical pot smoker. Bennett and White quote Seattle thoracic surgeon Eric Vallieres on that very point.

"Some argue that one or two joints per day of exposure to these carcinogens does not even come close to the 1–2 packs per day contact a cigarette smoker experiences," Vallieres writes. "While this may mathematically make sense, the fact is that we do not know of a safe level for such exposures." Vallieres thus concedes that any lung cancer risk from smoking marijuana, assuming one exists, would be much lower than the risk observed in tobacco smokers, even among daily users. Still, he says, that does not mean smoking marijuana is completely safe!

Bennett and White devote much of their book to that sort of bait and switch. Consider their slippery handling of the fact that alcohol and tobacco kill people much more often than marijuana does. According to the U.S. Centers for Disease Control and Prevention, alcohol plays a role in something like 88,000 deaths a year, while tobacco is associated with 480,000. Tellingly, there is no official death toll for marijuana, although it's reasonable to assume the number is greater than zero, if only because stoned drivers get into fatal crashes from time to time. "As for the higher death and damage rates attributed to alcohol and tobacco," Bennett and White write, "it is at present correct to say more deaths are caused by those two legal substances than by marijuana. It is also true that alcohol and tobacco are far more widely used because they are legal."

The implication is that if marijuana were as popular as alcohol or tobacco, the marijuana death toll would be in the neighborhood of half a million a year. But as Bennett and White inadvertently concede, the number of marijuana-related deaths is much smaller not just in absolute terms but as a percentage of users. Bennett and White say there are seven times as many drinkers as pot smokers in this country. If marijuana were as dangerous as alcohol, we would already be seeing more than 12,000 marijuana-related deaths per year. Bennett and White say there are three times as many cigarette smokers as cannabis consumers. If marijuana were as dangerous as tobacco, we would already be seeing more than 150,000 marijuana-related deaths a year.

Obviously this is absurd, as Bennett and White eventually admit: "The point is this: there is no level of marijuana use that is actually completely safe." Wasn't the point supposed to be that "marijuana is at least as harmful as tobacco and alcohol"?

Never mind. Having abandoned that prominently placed claim, Bennett and White instead argue that "marijuana use is not safe or harmless." That point is important, they say, because marijuana is "propagated as harmless (at worst) and therapeutic (at best)," and "the culture has convinced itself marijuana is harmless." Still, one might question the relevance of showing that marijuana is not harmless in light of the fact that "almost none of the supporters of legalization of marijuana claim that smoking marijuana is without risk." Maybe they realize something that Bennett and White do not.

Ultimately, the question is not whether marijuana use carries risks, or even whether its risks are smaller than those posed by alcohol and tobacco—although that point surely casts doubt on the rationality, consistency, and fairness of our drug laws, as Bennett and White hazily perceive. "While there are dangerous substances that are legal in America (like tobacco and alcohol), we would be very ill-advised to add one more dangerous product (marijuana) to the list of things Americans should freely be able to obtain and use," they write. "We can add to the menu of dangerous substances available to our citizens, or we can draw a line and admit we are surfeited with the problems that already exist."

That is the real crux of Bennett and White's argument, and it depends on accepting their premise that using force to stop people from hurting themselves is morally justified. In the case of marijuana prohibition, this use of force includes hundreds of thousands of arrests each year—nearly 700,000 in 2013, the vast majority (88 percent) for simple possession. "When there is an arrest for possession," Bennett and White claim, "it is usually of a large quantity—a lot of pounds." If that were true, there would be a lot more people accused of possession with intent to distribute and a lot fewer charged with simple possession. Bennett and White mention "one Department of Justice study" that "showed the median amount of marijuana seized in a possession arrest to be 115 pounds." That figure comes from a study of federal cases, which tend to involve large quantities but account for a tiny fraction of total marijuana arrests (around 1 percent).

Even as they inaccurately claim that people caught with marijuana typically have "a lot of pounds," Bennett and White also say the arrests are no big deal because they generally do not result in jail or prison sentences. Around 40,000 marijuana offenders nevertheless are serving sentences as long as life for growing a plant or distributing its produce. And even if cannabis consumers do not spend much time behind bars when they are busted, they still suffer the humiliation, cost, inconvenience, loss of liberty, stigma, and lasting ancillary penalties of a criminal arrest. That is no small thing, but Bennett and White shrug it off, likening marijuana possession to drunk driving, burglary, and theft. The fact that police arrest a lot of people for those offenses, they say, does not mean that drunk driving, burglary, and theft should be decriminalized. The crucial distinction, of course, is that marijuana in someone's pocket does not run over pedestrians, break into people's homes, or steal their wallets.

Bennett and White do not begin to grapple with the question of how it can be just to treat people as criminals when their actions violate no one's rights. They simply take it as a given that "the government not only has a right, but a duty to keep the public safe from harm, including dangerous substances." They maintain that an action is "worthy of being illegal" if it is "something that hurts individuals or society." Since Bennett has a Ph.D. in political philosophy, we can assume he understands the implications of his words, which make no distinction between self-regarding behavior and actions that harm others, or between the sort of injury that violates people's rights and the sort that does not. It would be hard to come up with a broader license for government intervention, and it is impossible to reconcile Bennett and White's free-ranging paternalism with their avowed support for "less government intrusion into the lives of all Americans."

Here is how Bennett and White sum up the moral objection to marijuana prohibition: "What is the ultimate right being argued for? ... At the end of the day the right is, simply put, a right to get and be stoned. This, it seems to us, is a rather ridiculous right upon which to charge a hill."

This is like saying that freedom of speech is the right to tweet about the latest episode of *American Idol*, or that freedom of religion is the right to believe silly things and engage in pointless rituals. It is true as far as it goes, but it overlooks the broader principle. Drug prohibition dictates to people what substances they may ingest and what states of consciousness they may seek, thereby running roughshod over the principle that every man is sovereign over his own body and mind.

Even if marijuana is not as bad as they portray it, Bennett and White ask, "Do we need it?" They think cannabis consumers need to justify their freedom, when it is prohibitionists who need to justify forcibly imposing their pharmacological preferences on others. After so many years of taking that power for granted, it is hardly surprising they are not up to the task.

1. Does Bennett and White's "prohibitionist screed" contain any points that might change hearts and minds, or is it simply preaching to the converted?

2. Do you find this review overly biased? After all, this is a book by the former drug czar...what would one expect?

"WINDS OF CHANGE BLOW IN POT ISSUE: AS LIKELY VOTE NEARS IN OHIO, SUPPORT COMES FROM UNLIKELY PLACES," BY LAURA A. BISCHOFF AND CHRIS STEWART, FROM *DAYTON DAILY NEWS*, MAY 17, 2015

No matter what happens to a proposed constitutional amendment to make marijuana legal in Ohio, polls show a growing acceptance for legalization in this country—including a majority who think recreational use of marijuana should be legal.

And the support is coming from unlikely corners. Hamilton County Prosecutor Joe Deters is a law-and-order Republican who has spent most of his career putting away bad guys in Ohio's third-largest county. But Deters, who announced last week that he'll head up a 10-person task force to look at the impact of legalization, is rethinking whether going after marijuana users is worth the public expense.

"I think that most of our marijuana laws are an incredible waste of resources," said Deters. The drug is easily obtained on the street, but users don't have the benefit of knowing exactly what's in it and the community doesn't benefit from the untaxed sales, he said.

Deters acknowledged that his fellow prosecutors may not share his views, but there is little doubt public opinion is moving toward his position.

Gallup has been polling Americans on marijuana legalization since 1969, when 12 percent thought it was a good idea. Just a few years ago, support for legalization inched across the 50 percent line, according to Gallup.

When people are asked about medical marijuana, their support increases dramatically.

A Quinnipiac University poll in April found 84 percent of Ohioans say they support allowing adults to legally use marijuana for medical purposes if a doctor prescribes it. The same poll found 52 percent support allowing adults to legally use small amounts for recreational use.

The proposed constitutional amendment would legalize marijuana for both recreational and medical use under certain conditions.

Deters says his experience as a prosecutor has led him to his changed views.

"I'm probably on the fringe, but I've been doing this for 33 years and I've seen how it unfairly impacts minorities," he said. "It's a low-level intoxicant compared to even alcohol and I just think we need to get in front of this, in front of what's coming to Ohio."

Robert Ryan, the Ohio president for the National Organization for the Reform of Marijuana Laws (NORML), recalls a meeting two years ago when Deters was peppered with questions from "crusty old businessmen" about the legalization of pot.

"He kind of danced around it, but at the time he said he was willing to talk about it," Ryan said. "Now, he's actually willing to say it."

Montgomery County Prosecutor Mat Heck said through a spokesman that he thinks marijuana legalization should be carefully reviewed. "Then after a thorough review is completed and the details have been provided, the voters will decide if they feel this proposal is appropriate for Ohio," he said.

Experts agree that Ohio spends millions of dollars enforcing marijuana laws, but no central clearinghouse keeps track.

"What we know anecdotally is, we're spending millions and we know the federal government is spending millions," said Ohio Public Defender Tim Young, who favors legalizing marijuana through legislation. Young argues that pot smokers typically do not get involved in crimes such as gun violence or burglary yet pay a huge price when they are arrested, which often includes the loss of their driver's license, which then affects whether they can go to school.

"It's devastating in terms of the consequences that are attached to this compared to what the public believes the harm is," he said.

Some in law enforcement caution against assuming marijuana is harmless, noting that violence is often associated with dealing in an unregulated black market.

"We have people who are shot and are killed in marijuana transactions or drug rip offs of those who traffic it because people know they have money," said Dayton

Police Chief Richard Biehl. "So we know the illegal market produces harm of that nature."

While some form of legalization might negate that violence, society will still have to deal with another set of potential problems, Biehl said.

"It doesn't come without public health consequences; it doesn't come without public safety consequences," he said. "What does one mean by legalization in terms of specifics? What is the level of social control? Like with tobacco, that's a legal substance and there's social regulation, community regulation of that. Without that refined detail, I think that anyone who offers an opinion will probably miss the mark."

Helen Jones-Kelley, executive director of the Alcohol, Drug Addiction and Mental Health Services Board for Montgomery County, said the board responsible for funding and planning addiction services in the county is not necessarily opposed to medical use of marijuana if it is approved and regulated by the Food and Drug Administration like other prescription drugs.

But Jones-Kelley is dead-set against legalizing recreational use of marijuana. "If we had to grapple with legalization of tobacco today, we would oppose that because now we know what happens," she said. "It's the same difference."

The pot amendment as written would benefit "a small group of people financially but will devastate the community," according to Jones-Kelley. "That's really troubling to us here because we will have the responsibility for helping pick up the pieces."

UNIQUE PERSPECTIVE

Brice Keller routinely took rocket fire in Iraq while guarding the gate to an Air Force base in Kirkuk. Later, as an investigator and police officer in Indiana, he fought in the "war on drugs," sometimes making undercover buys. His military and police experiences give him a unique perspective, Keller said. He admits to daily use of marijuana to help alleviate symptoms of post-traumatic stress syndrome. In his current profession as a criminal defense attorney, he sometimes represents clients facing pot possession charges.

"We're not supposed to have a class of criminals because they choose to medicate in a certain way, or use this plant in a certain way," he said. "It's just wrong."

As a police officer, Keller abused both alcohol and cigarettes and said he was "running 100 miles an hour all the time."

"I realized I'd get anxiety and all these other things that were related to PTSD and it would just build up," he said. "When you can smoke some marijuana you can calm down and get an appropriate amount of sleep and reduce urges toward heavy drinking or reduce urges to smoke cigarettes constantly."

Keller is a member of Law Enforcement Against Prohibition, a group of current and past police officers and criminal justice professionals who believe the "war on drugs" has largely been a failure and a government system of regulation and control would be more effective.

"In general, the idea is if we take drug abuse to be a civil problem instead of a criminal problem, then it renews trust and faith in the police," Keller said.

One of the arguments advanced by those who favor legalization is that it would free up police to focus more on serious crime.

Law enforcement posts high conviction rates on marijuana cases because they tend to be easy cases, said NORML's Ryan.

"People tend to do things that are easy," he said. "Solving a murder case is not easy. Solving a rape case is not easy."

Data from the Ohio Highway Patrol shows a dramatic increase in pot cases in recent years. The patrol had 44 marijuana trafficking cases in 2014, quadruple the number from seven years earlier. And patrol citations for marijuana possession hit 5,969 in 2014, up from 2,081 in 2009.

The Bureau of Criminal Identification and Investigation in the attorney general's office typically seizes 46,664 plants a year through its marijuana eradication program.

Montgomery County Sheriff Phil Plummer said enforcing current minor possession pot laws doesn't place any extra financial burden on the county because those citations are treated more like traffic tickets and no one is being transported or booked into jail. He's against legalizing pot for recreational use because he thinks it will increase the workload of his staff.

"If it becomes legal, we'll be arresting more people for OVI and handling more traffic crashes," said Plummer, who is also against legalization because he believes marijuana use leads to abuse of other drugs.

"I think it's a gateway drug. I don't think it's good to make it available to the children of our community and it's a huge public safety issue," Plummer said.

LAWMAKERS OPPOSE BALLOT ISSUE

Ohioans are expected to vote in November on whether to flip from a ban on pot to legalizing it for both medicinal and recreational purposes.

ResponsibleOhio, which is backed by deep-pocketed investors and experienced political consultants, is proposing a constitutional amendment to designate 10 sites its investors control as properties where marijuana can be legally manufactured. The campaign also wants to create an Ohio Marijuana Control Commission, allow adults 21 and older to home grow up to four plants, establish six testing centers to ensure quality and safety, and give local voters approval power over whether retail shops are allowed in their neighborhoods.

The campaign reported that it has already collected 320,000 signatures to place the question on the ballot. ResponsibleOhio needs to submit 305,591 valid signatures from registered voters by July 1 and then the campaign is expected to spend roughly $25 million to convince voters to say yes.

Opposing the issue are anti-drug groups and statewide officeholders, including Gov. John Kasich, Attorney General Mike DeWine, Secretary of State Jon Husted, Auditor Dave Yost, Treasurer Josh Mandel, and key legislative leaders including House Speaker Cliff Rosenberger, R-Clarksville, and Senate President Keith Faber, R-Celina.

Some state leaders vehemently object to carving commercial oligarchies into the state constitution, having already seen that happen with two companies naming four casino sites in the constitution.

State Rep. Mike Curtin, D-Marble Cliff, the former editor and associate publisher of the *Columbus Dispatch*, opposes legalizing marijuana and particularly opposes doing so via the Ohio Constitution.

"This issue is about the granting of a monopoly right in the Ohio Constitution. This issue is about prostituting the Ohio Constitution for personal financial enrichment," Curtin wrote to his colleagues last week. "I plan to play a very active role in the campaign to defeat this proposal and I hope you will join that effort."

Yost is calling on lawmakers to put a constitutional amendment on the fall ballot that would prohibit business interests from carving out monopolies or oligarchies via the state constitution. And Husted last week urged lawmakers to step in and consider a thoughtful way forward.

"The constitution shouldn't be somebody's paycheck," Yost testified.

Young, who favors legalization, agrees with Curtin and Yost that amending the constitution isn't the way to go about it. It's easier to tweak or change state law, he said.

"Absolutely, it should be legalized, but it should be done at the legislative level. Much the same way I say gambling should have been handled."

But Lydia Bolander, spokesperson for ResponsibleOhio, said Ohio lawmakers have failed to act on marijuana legalization since it was first introduced 18 years ago and they're out of step with Ohioans' views.

"In passing a constitutional amendment, voters are taking part in direct democracy, which is exactly why such a process exists," she said. "When the legislature fails to act, the people have a right to come together and take action."

Reprinted with permission from the Dayton Daily News and Cox Media Group Ohio.

1. Given the reality that marijuana arrests are "low hanging fruit" distracting the law enforcement community from more serious crimes, might decriminalization solve the problem? Or should those who medicate for PTSD and other ailments be subject to the same state laws as everyone else?

2. Lydia Bolander spins Issue 3 as an example of "direct democracy" in action, but opponents accuse those in favor of the initiative of trying to use a constitutional amendment to line their pockets. Which is closer to the truth, in your opinion?

CHAPTER 6

WHAT ORDINARY PEOPLE SAY

In America, the idea of "ordinary citizens" or "average Americans" is itself a fictional construct—generally taken to mean white, middle-class Christian folks in the so-called fly-over states. The term is usually deployed for rhetorical purposes. However, even if such a construct had a basis in real lives and concrete demographic data, it would still do little to help us sort through the issue of marijuana reform. Indeed, opinions on the subject defy most of the predictable ways in which people line-up politically, and have much to do with subjective experience and prejudices. What's more, the big money involved in marijuana legalization has made for some unusual alliances, as we've seen in Ohio.

Owing to her past struggle with dependence, writer Susan Shapiro urges cautious legalization, and rails against simple-minded veneration of stoner archetypes and celebrity tokers. A follow-up to Shapiro's original article describes the pro-pot community's hostility toward her following its publication.

The next selected article also urges caution in regard to marijuana reform. Returning home to Denver, Colorado following the institution of legalized recreational marijuana, reporter Marshall Allen cautions that it may take some time for the state to discover its own best practices in regard to public health and marijuana use.

We'll begin by looking at some statistical data recently compiled by the Pew Research Center, which shows unambiguously that the majority of Americans support legalized marijuana.

EXCERPT FROM "AMERICA'S NEW DRUG POLICY LANDSCAPE," FROM THE *PEW RESEARCH CENTER*, APRIL 2, 2014

SECTION 2: VIEWS OF MARIJUANA – LEGALIZATION, DECRIMINALIZATION, CONCERNS

Public support for legalizing marijuana use is at an all-time high of 54%, though it is virtually unchanged from last year (52%). There is even more agreement that people convicted of possessing small amounts of marijuana should not serve time in jail.

About three-quarters of Americans (76%) say that if marijuana use is not legalized, those who are convicted of possessing small amounts of marijuana should not serve jail time. Just 22% favor jail time for those convicted of minor marijuana possession.

Views of the legalization of marijuana remain divided along partisan, age, and ethnic lines. While support for legalization has increased by 15 points among both parties since 2010, Republicans continue to be far less likely than Democrats to favor legalization (39% vs. 63%). Opposition to legalization also is much higher among those 65 and older than younger people and among Hispanics than non-Hispanic whites or blacks.

However, majorities across nearly all partisan and demographic groups say possession of small amounts of marijuana should not result in jail time. The partisan differences in these opinions are relatively modest—79% of Democrats, 78% of independents, and 69% of Republicans do not think people convicted of having small amounts of marijuana should serve time in jail.

People who have tried marijuana are more likely than those who have not to oppose jail time for minor possession. Still, a majority of those who have never tried marijuana (63%) say people convicted of small amounts of marijuana should not spend time in jail. Among those who have tried marijuana, but not in the past year, 88% oppose jail time for possession of small amounts of marijuana, as do 97% of those who have used it in the past year.

RELATIVE DANGERS POSED BY ALCOHOL AND MARIJUANA

When asked which is more harmful to a person's health, 69% of Americans say alcohol, while just 15% consider marijuana to be more harmful. Similarly, 63% say that if marijuana were as widely available as alcohol, the latter would be more harmful to society; 23% say marijuana would do the most harm.

Majorities across most demographic groups say alcohol is more harmful than marijuana to a person's health and to society. But roughly a third of Hispanics (32%), people 65 and older (31%), and Republicans (36%) say marijuana would be more harmful to society than alcohol, if it were as widely available.

Even among those who say the use of marijuana by adults should not be legal, many consider alcohol to be more harmful to a person's health; 45% say this is the case, compared with 29% who think marijuana is more harmful. But those who say marijuana use should not be legal see it as more harmful to society: 51% marijuana say that if marijuana were as widely available as alcohol, it would be more harmful, while 32% say alcohol would be more harmful.

CONCERNS ABOUT MARIJUANA USE

While many support the legalization—or at least the decriminalization—of marijuana use, most (54%) say legalizing marijuana would lead to more underage people trying it.

Those ages 65 or older are particularly likely to say the legalization of marijuana would lead to more underage use; 69% in this group say this is the case, compared with about half of those in younger age groups.

Majorities of those who say marijuana use should be illegal and those who say it should only be legal for medicinal purposes are also more likely to say the legalization of marijuana would lead to more underage people trying it (80% and 66%, respectively). In contrast, just 29% of those who say marijuana should be legal for personal use say the same.

The view that legalizing marijuana would lead to more underage people trying it is also more prevalent among Republicans. About two-thirds of Republicans (66%) say this would happen, while about half of Democrats (48%) and independents (51%) agree.

SIX-IN-TEN WOULD BE BOTHERED BY PUBLIC USE OF MARIJUANA

Americans overwhelmingly say that if marijuana were legal, it would not bother them if people used marijuana in their own homes; 83% say this, including 60% of those who do not think marijuana use should be legal for personal or medicinal purposes.

But 63% would be bothered if people used marijuana in public, including a sizable minority (39%) of those who say marijuana use by adults should be legal for personal use.

Older Americans are particularly likely to say that if marijuana were legal, they would be bothered by people using it in public, but majorities across all age groups share this view. About three-quarters (76%) of those 65 or older would be bothered by marijuana use in public, as would 56% of those under 30, 60% of those 30–49 and 64% of 50- to 64-year-olds.

When asked if it would bother them if a store or business selling marijuana legally opened up in their neighborhood, about six-in-ten (57%) say they would not be bothered, but majorities of those who say marijuana use should not be legal (76%) and those who say it should only be legal for medicinal use (57%) would be bothered by this.

Hispanics are more likely than non-Hispanic whites and blacks to say it would bother them if a store of business selling marijuana opened up in their neighborhood; 51% of Hispanics say they would be bothered and 47% would not. In contrast, about six-in-ten whites (58%) and blacks (62%) would not be bothered by this.

1. Why might beliefs about the legalization of marijuana be "divided along partisan, age, and ethnic lines?

"CANNABIS CRAZY: IT'S DOESN'T JUST DESCRIBE THE MOVE TO LEGALIZE WEED, IT COULD HAPPEN TO YOU," BY SUSAN SHAPIRO, FROM THE *LOS ANGELES TIMES*, JANUARY 3, 2015

In 2014, our country went cannabis crazy, bringing to 18 the number of states decriminalizing pot. Colorado opened boutiques selling "mountain high suckers" in grape and butterscotch flavors and posted signs that proclaimed the state is "where prohibition ends and the fun begins." In my New York home, I'm glad that someone can carry up to 50 joints and no longer get thrown in the joint. Yet I worry that user-friendly laws and such recent screen glorifications as "High Maintenance" and "Kid Cannabis" send young people a message that getting stoned is cool and hilarious.

I know the dark side. I'm ambivalent about legalizing marijuana because I was addicted for 27 years. After starting to smoke weed at Bob Dylan concerts when I was 13, I saw how it can make you say and do things that are provocative and perilous. I bought pot in bad neighborhoods at 3 a.m., confronted a dealer for selling me a dime bag of oregano, let shady pushers I barely knew deliver marijuana, like pizza, to my home. I mailed weed to my vacation spots and smoked a cocaine-laced joint a bus driver offered when I was his only passenger.

Back then Willie Nelson songs, Cheech and Chong routines, and "Fast Times at Ridgemont High's" Jeff Spicoli made getting high seem kooky and harmless. My reality was closer to Walter White's self-destruction from meth on TV's "Breaking Bad" and the delusional nightmares in the film "Requiem for a Dream." Everyone believed you couldn't get addicted to pot.

Turns out I could get hooked on carrot sticks. Marijuana became an extreme addiction for me. I'm not alone. Nearly 17% of those who get high as teenagers will become addicted to marijuana, according to the 2013 edition of the Diagnostic and Statistical Manual of Mental Disorders. The 2012 National Survey on Drug Use and Health found that up to half of daily marijuana smokers become addicted—an estimated 2.7 million people in the U.S.

The years I toked, I struggled with love and work, sometimes feeling suicidal. The brilliant addiction specialist who helped me give up pot a dozen years ago taught me that addicts self-medicate because underlying every substance problem he'd ever seen "is a deep depression that feels unbearable." One-on-one therapy helped me untangle what I was getting wasted to escape. Being drug-free saved my health, marriage, and career. Within a year, my income tripled. I came to believe my doctor's adage: "When you quit a toxic habit you leave room for something beautiful to take its place."

In writing classes I teach in New York and L.A., students from many backgrounds confessed that they "smoked a bowl" or "got ripped" and then got in a car accident, fell on subway tracks, had a wallet or cellphone stolen, were sexually assaulted, or had a physical altercation that landed them in the hospital or jail. My undergraduates loved the series "Weeds" and "Harold & Kumar" films and joked about being "cross-faded," simultaneously imbibing on alcohol and marijuana.

Yet I warn them that getting stoned greatly increases the likelihood of something bad happening, reminding them that pot blurs reality, reduces inhibitions—and regularly leads to tragedy. Consider two deaths in 2014 in Colorado that police linked to pot: a 47-year-old man who ate marijuana-infused candy and fatally shot his wife, and a 19-year-old student who ingested a marijuana cookie and jumped to his death.

The weed of today is far stronger than in the past. President Obama admitted smoking marijuana as a teen and said it's no worse than alcohol but hopes his daughters will avoid "the bad habit." The new edible pot products can be 10 times stronger than a traditional joint, says a report in the *New England Journal of Medicine*. The strength of pot varies, and it's impossible to predict its effect. How you react to marijuana depends on your size, what you've eaten, the medications you take. As I tapered off, one hit from a pipe or bong could leave me reeling, as if I'd had five drinks.

Marijuana use doubles the risk of being in a car accident if you drive soon after smoking it, and it causes more car accidents than any other illicit drugs, according to Columbia University researchers. They found it contributed to 12% of traffic deaths in the U.S. in 2010, triple the rate of a decade earlier.

The medical side effects are also significant. Smoking pot increases the risk of lung cancer 8%, according to British and New Zealand studies. It's associated with bronchitis, respiratory infections, and increases the risk of heart attack and stroke, concluded a New England Journal study. Another 2014 study found frequent use by teenagers and young adults causes cognitive decline and decreases IQ. Marijuana essentially fries your brain.

Being a stoner was easy. Quitting was hard but gave me more to live for. Before jumping on the buzzed bandwagon in the new year, throwing a pot dessert party or voting to lift all restrictions across the nation, ask yourself and your kids: Is the high worth the lows? We shouldn't send pot smokers to prison, but they don't belong on pop-culture pedestals either.

1. Do you feel the author's claim she could "get hooked on carrot sticks" undermines the credibility of her argument?

2. Does pop culture put marijuana "on a pedestal" as the author claims, or does it simply represent how people actually behave, regardless of legality?

"CANNABIS CRAZY," BY SUSAN SHAPIRO, FROM *NEWSDAY*, FEBRUARY 2, 2015

Critics in California and Oregon have labeled me another prohibitionist attempting to slander the sacred herb, Nancy Reagan, a DEA agent, the church lady in Reefer Madness, and a born-again Christian proselytizer. Funny names for a left-wing Jewish liberal from New York who argues against jailing anyone for smoking joints.

Why? Because I publicly lamented the glamorization of ganja on the Web series "High Maintenance" and the comedy film "Kid Cannabis"—both of which make pot smoking look like hilarious fun. I maligned the touting of Colorado boutiques selling "mountain high suckers" in rainbow flavors of weed, like candy, that could attract children. Furthermore, I challenged pro-marijuana spins that insist pot is completely nonaddictive and harmless.

Mostly, I confessed that getting high at 13 got me hooked on pot for decades—until an addiction specialist helped me stop at 41, explaining, "When you quit a toxic substance, you leave room for something beautiful to take its place." Indeed, in the last dozen years toke-free, I've fixed my career and my marriage and tripled my income.

Thus I acknowledged my ambivalence about the fervent legalization campaign across the country, fearing pot could be dangerous for young people, based on statistics, reports from *The New England Journal of Medicine*, troubling stories from my students and my own bad experiences.

To be clear: I have no problem with medical marijuana and feel nobody should be imprisoned for recreational toking. I hope smoke-able weed is legalized in all 50 states, but only with restrictions similar to those for alcohol and cigarettes: prohibited under age 18 or 21, not sold in vending machines and dispensed in regulated doses. After all, about 17 percent of those who get high as teens will become addicted to marijuana (like I was), along with up to half of people who smoke pot daily, according to the definition of addiction in The Diagnostic and Statistical Manual of Mental Disorders. The 2012 National Survey on Drug Use and Health shows 2.7 million people over age 12 fit the criteria for marijuana addiction.

I worry commercialized edible cannabis can be perilous because reactions vary and doses are confusing. Even Pulitzer Prize–winning columnist Maureen Dowd mistakenly ate too much pot candy—in the form of a caramel-chocolate candy bar—and nearly overdosed. If she couldn't figure out what amount was safe to ingest, how could your average teenager?

I have analyzed the hostility surrounding this hot-button personal freedom issue. Maybe a gray slant by

CRITICAL PERSPECTIVES ON LEGALIZING MARIJUANA

a former user like myself is threatening in a long black-and-white war that tokers feel they are close to winning. I knew I was in trouble when a Shreveport ACLU director trashed me while I was defended by a Louisiana Republican MD and U.S. Representative. (My staid doctor dad in Florida was shocked we finally agreed on something.)

I felt vindicated, yet saddened, when many others—of all backgrounds—recently shared stories about the dark side of pot:

A Southern grandma is heartbroken that her beloved granddaughter became a lethargic pothead who dropped out of school and isn't working.

A Northwest widow believes smoking marijuana for 40 years exacerbated her husband's denial of and horrible death from lung cancer.

A sister is convinced her brother's life and artistic talent were destroyed by weed, which he smoked since age 15, leading to debilitating paranoia and dementia.

While addiction is defined by "a compulsive need for a substance," my addiction specialist says that to tell if something is a habit or addictive behavior, just quit for a week. If you have no problem, you probably weren't addicted.

Based on all the kooky cannabis commentary, I wouldn't want to witness the West Coast's withdrawal symptoms.

1. Why does the author state she felt she needed to write this follow-up piece to her original article?

2. Do you think that the "kooky cannabis commentary" the author laments in this article shows that cannabis's most fervent supporters might be driven by their own addictions rather than thinking about the general good?

"ROCKY MOUNTAIN HIGH OR REEFER MADNESS? LEGAL POT IN COLORADO COMES WITH RISKS," BY MARSHALL ALLEN, FROM *PROPUBLICA*, APRIL 7, 2014

A REPORTER RETURNS TO HIS HOMETOWN AND CONFRONTS THE NEW REALITY OF LEGALIZED MARIJUANA.

This story was co-published with The Denver Post's The Cannabist

I walked through clouds of marijuana smoke Friday night to get to the Denver Nuggets basketball game. The sweet smell lingering in the air reminded me less of a family event and more of the time I saw AC/DC on "The Razor's Edge" tour at the old McNichols Sports Arena.

I grew up in Colorado, but it's been a while since I lived in the state. When I returned for a recent conference, I found that a place settled by the Gold Rush is now mad about reefer. In 2012, Colorado voters became the first in the nation to approve recreational pot use. The good times rolled out Jan. 1, when stores started selling it.

I've never tried pot, but I graduated from the University of Colorado—Boulder, which is famous for its annual "4/20" public pot parties. At CU, you can practically get a contact high walking to class. But I saw more public pot use in my two-day visit to Lower Downtown Denver than in years spent at Boulder.

It's supposed to be illegal to smoke or consume pot in public. But then the day after the game, while jogging down the Speer Boulevard bike path, I passed a guy lounging under a tree lavishing his affections on a joint.

Anyone over 21 can walk into a dispensary and load up on bud, marijuana baked goods, and candy.

The presence of legal pot right outside our hotel made people giddy at the conference I attended—a meeting of the Association of Health Care Journalists. At a reception, one woman passed a friend gummy bears infused with THC, or *tetrahydrocannabinol*, the main psychoactive ingredient in pot.

And then there was a friend of mine at the conference—I'll call him "Dude" because he shared his story on condition I didn't name him. He had a bad reaction after eating too many marijuana gummy bears.

There's a running debate about whether pot should be legal for recreational use, but the Colorado experiment is rapidly unfolding, and it could help determine whether other states follow or shy away. (Washington voters also have approved recreational marijuana, and the state expects to begin licensing retailers in July.)

Two things stand out after my visit.

First, legal pot is attracting new and possibly naïve users—creating risks that some don't bargain for. Second, the public health system's desire to protect people may be well-intentioned, but regulation and efforts to track the health effects have a ways to go.

Dude had only smoked pot twice in his life, about 25 years ago, but he got curious and tried some pot gummy bears from a shop called the LoDo Wellness Center. Other than being infused with THC they looked and tasted like ordinary candy. Dude and his buddy paid $20 for a pack of 10.

Dude ate a bear before dinner but felt nothing. So he popped another during the meal. Nada. *Ripoff*, he assumed. So he ate a few more — five total, he said — but still felt nothing. He fell asleep in his hotel room at 11 p.m.

Two hours later, Dude awoke feeling like he was on a roller coaster. His entire body tingled, and he was light headed. He tried to stand, but his left leg was so numb he couldn't walk to the bathroom. His pounding heart strained his rib cage as waves of euphoria and anxiety washed over him.

He was terrified.

Was this the high? An overdose? A heart attack? A stroke?

Totally debilitated, Dude thought about calling an ambulance but feared ending up in the E.R. or a police station. So he stayed put, guzzled water, pulled a blanket over his head, and clutched a pillow. The symptoms lasted two hours, but it took a full day to feel normal again.

Dude's experience and the open pot use I saw made me wonder about public health aspect of legalization. I called some experts to find out if there have been safety problems, how pot and gummy bears are being regulated and whether consumers are being educated about the risks.

The foods with pot—typically baked goods but also sodas, candies and even lasagna and pizza—cause the most unpredictable highs because the effects aren't immediate and potency varies, I learned.

In the case of gummy bears, one is considered a single serving. But Dude kept eating them because he didn't feel anything.

Haley Andrews, manager of the LoDo Wellness Center, said about half the shop's customers are marijuana novices, so the staff takes time to educate everyone who buys. Users should start with one 10 mg gummy bear, she said, and never consume more than 20 mg at a time.

Andrews said the gummy bear bottle's label listed the number of 10 mg servings inside and advises users to consume with caution because the product had not been tested for contaminants or potency. There is no mention of a delayed response, she said.

The *Denver Post* recently tested edibles and found that potency labeling was often inaccurate.

Accurate or not, labels are often ignored.

Dude said his buddy held onto the package so he never looked at it. He claims no one at the shop gave him any warnings about the gummy bears.

There were signs in the shop about how the different strains of pot would make users feel—"calm" or "excited"—but Dude said he saw no displays with advice for novice users, how many gummy bears are too many, or warnings about a delayed response.

Andrews said the staff makes every effort to ensure people use the products safely, but that it's possible Dude somehow slipped through the cracks.

Generally, using too much pot isn't life-threatening. But a reaction like Dude's could contribute to a heart attack or stroke for someone who has health problems, said Dr. Tista Ghosh of the Colorado Department of Public Health. She said recreational pot has been unexpectedly popular with the older crowd.

"There's a lot we don't know," Ghosh said. "I feel like in some ways we're like tobacco 50 years ago. More research needs to be done on this from the public health and individual health perspective."

Looking back on it, Dude said he was glad to be in his hotel room when the reaction hit him and not in a place where he could endanger others. According to reports in the Denver Post, pot use has contributed to car crashes and the recent death of a Wyoming college student, who on a spring break visit to Denver, began acting strangely and jumped from a fourth-floor hotel balcony.

Though ruled an accident, a coroner's report said "marijuana intoxication" from eating several pot cookies was a significant contributor to the 19-year-old's death, the *Post* reported.

Children are especially at risk. It's illegal to make candy or fruit-flavored cigarettes in the United States, but pot candies and cookies in Colorado have been some of the best-selling products. Although the packaging is child-proof, it doesn't stop kids once it's open.

Dr. Andrew Monte, a medical toxicologist at the University of Colorado Medical School and Rocky Mountain Poison and Drug Center, didn't have hard numbers but estimated that there is a poison control call every few days about a child accidentally eating marijuana products.

There also are reports from emergency room doctors, though no official numbers yet, of children showing up to hospitals in extreme states of drowsiness after accidentally consuming THC products, Monte said. Some end up getting expensive diagnostic work-ups like CT scans and spinal taps, he said.

"What kid doesn't want a brownie or a gummy bear?" Monte said.

So far, there are no mandatory tests of the potency or purity of recreational pot or THC food products, but they are scheduled to roll out in the coming months under the rules to implement the new law.

The process is more complicated than it would be in other cases because state regulators have not been able to rely on the federal health agencies. The federal government deems marijuana an illegal substance, so it's not participating in the oversight, Ghosh said.

Ghosh said the Colorado regulators have had to start some things from scratch, including finding labs that can be certified to test pot products.

Michael Elliott, executive director of the Marijuana Industry Group, which represents marijuana centers, growers, and infused products manufacturers in Colorado, said there are clean kitchen standards in place now, and licensing of facilities, financial disclosures, security, and more.

He said the industry is committed to robust regulation.

Elliott, Ghosh, and Monte agree that more needs to be done to educate consumers.

The state has put up a website with information about the law and advice for parents and is running a "Drive High, Get a DUI" campaign, efforts that Elliott says are supported by the marijuana industry.

Included on the website is a page titled "Using Too Much?" aimed at people like Dude.

Public health also depends on people using common sense. My friend Dude is a smart guy, but he knows he was a dumb consumer when he gobbled the pot gummy bears. Now, he regrets assuming that because marijuana was legal nothing could go wrong.

"I was ignorant about the whole thing," he told me later. "I am embarrassed to admit that I just ate the gummy bears because it seemed like fun.

"It was not."

1. Do you think the issues detailed in this article about recreational marijuana use in Colorado are solely due to the newness of the law and, thus, will gradually be resolved? Or do you think they are symptomatic of the larger public health issues of pot use?

CONCLUSION

In the twenty years since California voters approved the Compassionate Use Act, a ballot initiative legalizing medical marijuana use, public opinion has steadily shifted toward a more tolerant view of marijuana use. Popular depictions of marijuana have come a long way since the days of *Reefer Madness* (1936), and now routinely show casual cannabis use across all walks of life. According to polling, a majority of Americans support legalization, and do not believe pot is more harmful than alcohol.

In 2012, this trend culminated with the state of Colorado ending prohibition and creating the first legal market for recreational cannabis. Other states followed suit—marijuana is now legal in Alaska, Colorado, Washington, Oregon, and the District of Columbia. In the remainder of this decade, we can expect to see legalization in many more states, and possible laws to decriminalize the drug at the federal level as well.

Experts agree that increasingly widespread legal marijuana is inevitable. For these analysts, the question becomes how best to regulate an emerging billion-dollar industry to capitalize on its benefits and reduce its potential harms. Critics disagree, citing marijuana's effect on adolescent brain development and links to mental illness. Although all but the staunchest anti-legalization groups oppose retrenchment of a long since discredited and arguably racist drug war, moderates on both sides worry about a powerful corporate marijuana industry.

Ironically, pot's illegal status has prevented the gathering of accurate information about the drug, scientific and otherwise. As marijuana enters the legal market, we can expect new information to multiply. Thus, an informed account of marijuana reform is essential to an educated position. We hope this book has provided just that.

BIBLIOGRAPHY

Allen, Marshall. "Rocky Mountain High or Reefer madness? Legal Pot in Colorado Comes With Risks." *ProPublica*, April 7, 2014. Retrieved April 13, 2016 (https://www.propublica.org/article/rocky-mountain-high-or-reefer-madness-legal-pot-in-colorado-comes-with-risk#).

"America's New Drug Policy Landscape." *Pew Research Center.* April 2, 2014. Retrieved December 9, 2015 (www.people-press.org/2014/04/02/americas-new-drug-policy-landscape).

Bischoff, Laura A. and Christ Stewart. "Winds of Change Blow in Pot Issue: As Likely Vote Nears In Ohio, Support Comes From Unlikely Places." *Dayton Daily News*, May 17, 2015.

Dresser, Rebecca. "Irrational Basis: The Legal Status of Medical Marijuana." *The Hastings Center Report*, November/December. 2009. Retrieved December 9, 2015 (www.thehastingscenter.org/Publications/HCR/Detail.aspx?id=4118).

Frum, David. "Don't Go to Pot: The Case Against the Legalization of Marijuana." *Commentary*, October 2014. Retrieved December 9, 2015 (www.commentarymagazine.com/articles/dont-go-to-pot).

Hickenlooper, John. "Experimenting with Pot: The State of Colorado's Legalization of Marijuana." *The Milbank Quarterly*, Vol. 92, No. 2, 2014, pp. 243–249.

Kleiman, Mark. "How Not to Make a Hash Out of Cannabis Legalizaton." *Washington Monthly*, March/April/May 2014. Retrieved December 9, 2015 (www.washingtonmonthly.com/magazine/march_april_may_2014/features/how_not_to_make_a_hash_out_of049291.php?page=all).

Moody, Chris. "A Day in the Life of a Marijuana Lobbyist." *Yahoo News*, March 17, 2014. Retrieved April 13, 2016 (https://www.yahoo.com/news/a-day-in-the-life-of-a-marijuana-lobbyist-023347656.html?ref=gs).

Murray, Robin M. "Marijuana and Madness: Clinical Implications of Increased Availability and Potency." *Psychiatric Times*, Apr. 2015: 20. General One File. Web. 22 Oct. 2015.

NORML Board of Directors, "Principles Governing Responsible Cannabis Regulation." *NORML.com,* September 5, 2015.
Retrieved December 9, 2015 (norml.org/about/intro/item/prin-
ciples-governing-responsible-cannabis-regulation).

NORML Board of Directors, "Principles of Responsible Cannabis
Use." *NORML.com,* February 3, 1996. Retrieved December 9,
2015 (norml.org/principles/item/principles-of-responsible-can-
nabis-use-3).

Office of National Drug Control Policy. "Marijuana Myths and
Facts." Retrieved April 13, 2016 (https://www.ncjrs.gov/ondcp-
pubs/publications/pdf/marijuana_myths_facts.pdf)

Office of National Drug Control Policy. "Response to the *New
York Times* Editorial Board's Call for Medical Marijuana
Legalization." *WhiteHouse.gov*, July 28, 2014. Retrieved April
13, 2016 (https://www.whitehouse.gov/blog/2014/07/28/
response-new-york-times-editorial-boards-call-federal-mari-
juana-legalization).

SAM (Smart Approaches To Marijuana). "Legalization." Retrieved
December 9, 2015 (learnaboutsam.org/the-issues/legalization/).

SAM (Smart Approaches to Marijuana). "Scorecard of 2016 Presidential Candidates." October 29, 2015. Retrieved December 9,
2015 (learnaboutsam.org/wp-content/uploads/2015/10/29Oct20
15-SAM-presidential-scorecard-updated-for-distribution.pdf).

Shapiro, Susan. "An Ex-Pothead's Qualms About Legal Marijuana." *Newsday*, February 2, 2015. Retrieved December 30,
2015 (http://www.newsday.com/opinion/oped/a-ex-pothead-s-
qualms-about-legal-marijuana-susan-shapiro-1.9881702).

Shapiro, Susan. "Cannabis Crazy: It's Doesn't Just Describe the
Move to Legalize Weed, It Could Happen to You." *Los Angeles
Times*, January 3, 2015. Retrieved December 9, 2015 (http://
www.latimes.com/opinion/op-ed/la-oe-shapiro-marijuana-dan-
ger-20150104-story.html).

Street Law, Inc. *"Gonzales v. Raich* Case Summary." 2005. Retrieved
December 9, 2015 (www.streetlaw.org/document/119).

Sullum, Jacob. "Bill Bennett's Pot Prevarications: A Former Drug Czar's Dazed and Confused Defense of Marijuana Prohibition." *Reason*, May 2015. Retrieved December 9, 2015 (reason. com/archives/2015/05/01/bill-bennetts-pot-prevaricatio).

Warf, Curren and Alain Joffe. "Response to the American Academy of Pediatrics Report on Legalization of Marijuana." *Pediatrics*, November 2005:116:5. Web. 9 Dec. 2015.

CHAPTER NOTES

CHAPTER 1: WHAT THE EXPERTS SAY

"MARIJUANA AND MADNESS: CLINICAL IMPLICATIONS OF INCREASED AVAILABILITY AND POTENCY," BY ROBIN M. MURRAY

1. Hall W. What has research over the past two decades revealed about the adverse health effects of recreational cannabis use? *Addiction*. 2015;110:19–35.
2. Silins E, Horwood LJ, Patton GC, et al; Cannabis Cohorts Research Consortium. Young adult sequelae of adolescent cannabis use: an integrative analysis. *Lancet Psychiatry*. 2014; 1:286–293.
3. Solowij N. Cannabis and Cognitive Functioning. Cambridge, UK: *Cambridge University Press*; 1998.
4. Casadio P, Fernandes C, Murray RM, Di Forti M. Cannabis use in young people: the risk for schizophrenia. *Neurosci Biobehav Rev*. 2011;35:1779–1787.
5. Andreasson S, Allebeck P, Engstrom A, Rydberg U. Cannabis and schizophrenia: a longitudinal study of Swedish conscripts. *Lancet*. 1987;2:1483–1486.
6. Arseneault L, Cannon M, Poulton R, et al. Cannabis use in adolescence and risk for adult psychosis: longitudinal prospective study. *BMJ*. 2002;325:1212–1213.
7. Fergusson DM, Horwood LJ, Ridder EM. Tests of causal linkages between cannabis use and psychotic symptoms. *Addiction*. 2005;100:354–366.
8. Morrison PD, Zois V, McKeown DA, et al. The acute effects of synthetic intravenous Delta9-tetrahydrocannabinol on psychosis, mood and cognitive functioning. *Psychol Med*. 2009;39:1607–1616.
9. Potter DJ, Clark P, Brown MB. Potency of delta 9-THC and other cannabinoids in cannabis in England in 2005: implications for psychoactivity and pharmacology. *J Forensic Sci*. 2008;53:90–94.
10. Murray RM, Morrison PD, Henquet C, Di Forti M. Cannabis, the mind and society: the hash realities. *Nat Rev Neurosci*. 2007;8:885–895.
11. van Laar M, Cruts G, van Ooyen-Houben M, et al. Trimbos Institute. Report to the EMCDDA by the Reitox National

Focal Point: The Netherlands Drug Situation 2014. http://www. trimbos.nl/~7media/ files/gratis%20downloads/af1367%20the% 20netherlands%20drug%20situation%202014% 20a4-web.ashx. Accessed March 17, 2015.

12. Mehmedic Z, Chandra S, Slade D, et al. Potency trends of A9-THC and other cannabinoids in confiscated cannabis preparations from 1993 to 2008. *J Forensic Sci.* 2010;55:1209–1217.

13. Englund A, Morrison PD, Nottage J, et al. Cannabidiol inhibits THC-elicited paranoid symptoms and hippocampal-dependent memory impairment. *J Psychopharmacol.* 2013;27:19–27.

14. Di Forti M, Marconi A, Carra E, et al. Proportion of patients in south London with first-episode psychosis attributable to use of high potency cannabis: a case-control study. *Lancet Psychiatry.* February 18, 2015. http://www.thelancet.com/pb/assets/raw/ Lancet/pdfs/14TLP0454_Di%20Forti.pdf. Accessed March 17, 2015.

15. Morgan CJ, Curran HV. Effects of cannabidiol on schizophrenia-like symptoms in people who use cannabis. *Br J Psychiatry.* 2008;192:306–307.

16. Winstock AR, Barratt MJ. Synthetic cannabis: a comparison of patterns of use and effect profile with natural cannabis in a large global sample. *Drug Alcohol Depend.* 2013;131:106–111.

17. Pope HG Jr, Gruber AJ, Hudson JI, et al. Early-onset cannabis use and cognitive deficits: what is the nature of the association? *Drug Alcohol Depend.* 2003;69:303–310.

18. Meier MH, Caspi A, Ambler A, et al. Persistent cannabis users show neuropsychological decline from childhood to midlife. *Proc Natl Acad Sci U S A.* 2012;109:E2657–E2664.

19. Battistella G, Fornari E, Annoni JM, et al. Long-term effects of cannabis on brain structure *Neuropsychopharmacology.* 2014;39:2041–2048.

"RESPONSE TO THE AMERICAN ACADEMY OF PEDIATRICS REPORT ON LEGALIZATION OF MARIJUANA," BY CURREN WARF

1. Joffe A, Yancy WS; American Academy of Pediatrics Committee on Substance Abuse; American Academy of Pediatrics Committee on Adolescence. Legalization of marijuana: potential

impact on youth. Pediatrics. 2004;113(6). Available at: www.
pediatrics.org/cgi/content/full/113/6/e632
2. Deglamorising cannabis [commentary]. *Lancet*. 1995;346:1241
doi:10.1542/peds.2005–0128

"IN REPLY," BY ALAIN JOFFE

1. Compton WM, Grant BF, Coniver JD, Glantz MD, Stinson FS.
   Prevalence of marijuana use disorders in the United States:
   1991–1992 and 2001–2002. *JAMA*. 2004;291:2114–2121
2. Chambers RA, Taylor JR, Potenza MN. Developmental neurocir-
   cuitry of motivation in adolescence: a critical period of addiction vulnerability. *Am J Psychiatry*. 2003;160:1041–1052
3. Pistis M, Perra S, Pillolla G, Melis M, Muntoni AL, Gessa GL.
   Adolescent exposure to cannabinoids induces long-lasting
   changes in the response to drugs of abuse of rat midbrain
   dopamine neurons. *Biol Psychiatry*. 2004; 56:86–94.
4. Stefanis NC, Delespaul P, Henquet C, Bakoula C, Stefanis CN,
   Van Os J. Early adolescent cannabis exposure and positive and
   negative dimensions of psychosis. *Addiction*. 2004;99:1333–
   1341.
5. Fergusson DM, Horwood LJ, Swain-Campbell N. Cannabis use
   and psychosocial adjustment in adolescence and young adulthood. *Addiction*. 2002;97:1123–1135
6. Arseneault L, Cannon M, Poulton R, Murray R, Caspi A, Moffitt
   TE. Cannabis use in adolescence and risk for adult psychosis:
   longitudinal prospective study. *BMJ*. 2002;325:1212–1213.
7. Zammit S, Allebeck P, Andreasson S, Lundberg I, Lewis G.
   Self reported cannabis use as a risk factor for schizophrenia
   in Swedish conscripts of 1969: historical cohort study. *BMJ*.
   2002;325:1199.
8. Patton GC, Coffey C, Carlin JB, Degenhardt L, Lynskey M, Hall
   W. Cannabis use and mental health in young people: cohort
   study. *BMJ*. 2002;325:1195–1198.

CHAPTER 2: WHAT THE GOVERNMENT AND POLITICIANS SAY

"EXPERIMENTING WITH POT: THE STATE OF COLORADO'S LEGALIZATION OF MARIJUANA," BY JOHN HICKENLOOPER

1. A liberal drift. *The Economist.* November 10, 2012. http://www. economist.com/news/united-states/21565972-local-votessug-gest-more-tolerant countrybut-not-more-left-wing-oneliberal-drift. Accessed March 11, 2014.
2. Harkinson, J. Will your state be next to legalize pot? *Mother Jones.* February 7, 2014. http://www.motherjones.com/poli-tics/2014/02/ pot-marijuana-legalization-map-states. Accessed March 11, 2014.
3. Amendment 64 Implementation Task Force. Task force report on the implementation of Amendment 64: regulation of mari-juana in Colorado. http://www.colorado.gov/cms/forms/dortax/ A64TaskForceFinalReport.pdf. Published March 13, 2013. Accessed March 11, 2014.
4. Overview of Amendment 64. Campaign to Regulate Marijuana Like Alcohol website. http://www.regulatemarijuana.org/about. Accessed March 11, 2014.
5. Colorado Department of Revenue. Marijuana Enforcement Division 1CCR 212–2: permanent rules related to the Colorado retail marijuana code. http://www.colorado.gov/cs/Satellite?c= Document_C&childpagename=Rev-MMJ%2FDocument_C% 2FCBONAddLinkView&cid=1251646149281&pagename= CBON-Wrapper. Published September 9, 2013. Accessed March 11, 2014.
6. Colorado Department of Public Health and Environ-ment. FAQS: health effects of marijuana. http://www. colorado.gov/cs/Satellite? blobcol=urldata&blob-hea-dername1=Content-Disposition& blobheaderna-me2=ContentType&blobheadervalue1=inline% 3B±file-name%3D%22Marijuana±Health±Effects±FAQs.pdf% 22&blobheadervalue2=application%2Fpdf&blobkey=id& blobtable=MungoBlobs&blobwhere=1251941551125&ssbinary =true. Accessed March 11, 2014.

7. Tetrault JM, Crothers K, Moore BA, Mehra R, Concato J, Feillin DA. Effects of marijuana smoking on pulmonary function and respiratory complications: a systematic review. *Arch Intern Med.* 2007;167(3):221–228.
8. Paul, M. Marijuana users have abnormal brain structure and poor memory [news release]. Evanston, IL: *Northwestern University*; December 16, 2013. http://www.northwestern.edu/ newscenter/ stories/2013/12/marijuana-users-have-abnormal-brain-structure-- poor-memory.html. Accessed March 11, 2014.
9. Meier MH, Caspi A, Amber A, et al. Persistent cannabis users show neuropsychological decline from childhood to midlife. *PNAS.* August 27, 2012. doi:10.1073/pnas.1206820109.
10. Hickenlooper JW. Governor Hickenlooper's Amendment 64 and Proposition AA Implementation Budget Request. February 18, 2014. http://www.colorado.gov/cs/Satellite?blobcol=urldata& blobheader=application%2Fpdf&blobkey=id&blobtable= MungoBlobs&blobwhere=1251943287907&ssbinary=true. Accessed March 17, 2014.

EXCERPTS FROM "MARIJUANA MYTHS AND FACTS: THE TRUTH BEHIND 10 POPULAR MISPERCEPTIONS," FROM THE OFFICE OF NATIONAL DRUG CONTROL POLICY

1. National Survey on Drug Use and Health 2002: National Findings. Department of Health and Human Services, Substance Abuse and Mental Health Services Administration (SAMHSA), 2003.
2. Trends in Initiation of Substance Use, Substance Abuse and Mental Health Services Administration, based on the 2002 National Survey on Drug Use and Health. *SAMHSA*, 2003.
3. Marijuana Potency Monitoring Project, report No. 83. University of Mississippi, 2003.
4. Pope, HG and Yurelun Todd, D. The residual cognitive effects of heavy marijuana use in college students. *Journal of the American Medical Association*. 275(7): 521–527, 1996.

5. Pope, HG and Yurelun Todd, D. The residual cognitive effects of heavy marijuana use in college students. *Journal of the American Medical Association.* 275(7): 521–527, 1996.
6. Block, RI and Ghoneim, MM. Effects of chronic marijuana use on human cognition. *Psychopharmacology.* 110(12):219–228, 1993.
7. Herkenham, M et al. Cannabinoid receptor localization in the brain. Proceedings of the National Academy of Sciences of the United States of America. 87: 1932–1936, 1990. Mathew, RJ; Wilson, WH; Turkington, TG; and Coleman, RE. Cerebellar activity and disturbed time sense after THC. Brain Research. 797(2): 183–189, 1998.
8. Rodriguez de Fonseca, F et al. Activation of corticotrophin-releasing factor in the limbic system during cannabinoid withdrawal. *Science.* 276(5321): 2050–2064, 1997. Diana, M et al. Mesolimbic dopaminergic decline after cannabinoid withdrawal. Proceedings of the National Academy of Sciences of the United States of America. 95 (17): 10269–10273, 1998. MARIJUANA MARIJUANA myths & FACTS 27.
9. Herkenham, M et al. Cannabinoid receptor localization in the brain. Proceedings of the National Academy of Sciences of the United States of America. 87:1932–1936, 1990. 10 Brook, JS et al. The effect of early marijuana use on later anxiety and depressive symptoms. *NYS Psychologist.* 35–39, 2001.
10. Green, BE and Ritter, C. Marijuana use and depression. *Journal of Health and Social Behavior.* 41(1):40–49, 2000. Brook, JS et al. Longitudinal study of cooccurring psychiatric disorders and substance use. *Journal of the Academy of Child and Adolescent Psychiatry.* 37:322–330, 1998.
11. Greenblatt, J. Adolescent self-reported behaviors and their association with marijuana use. Based on data from the National Household Survey on Drug Abuse, 1994–1996 *SAMHSA,* 1998.
12. Bovasso, GB. Cannabis abuse as a risk factor for depressive symptoms. *American Journal of Psychiatry.* 158:2033–2037, 2001. Rey, J and Tennant, C. Cannabis and Mental Health (letter). *British Medical Journal* 325:1183–1184; 1212–1213, 2002. Zammit, S et al. Self reported cannabis use as a risk factor for schizophrenia in Swedish conscripts of 1969: historical cohort study. *British Medical Journal* 325:1199–1201, 2002.
13. National Survey on Drug Use and Health 2002. *SAMHSA,* 2003.

14. Brook, JS et al. Logitudinal study of co-occurring psychiatric disorders and substance use. *Journal of the American Academy of Child and Adolescent Psychiatry*. 37:322–330, 1998.

15. National Highway Traffic Safety Administration (NHTSA) Notes. Marijuana and alcohol combined severely impede driving performance. *Annals of Emergency Medicine*. 35:398–400, 2000.

16. Soderstrom, CA et al. Marijuana and other drug use among automobile and motorcycle drivers treated at a trauma center. Accident Analysis and Prevention. 25: 131–135, 1995. 28 MARIJUANA MARIJUANA myths & FACTS .

17. Substance Abuse and Mental Health Services Administration, Office of Applied Studies, National Survey on Drug Use and Health, 2002.

18. Gfroerer, JC and Wu, LT. Initiation of marijuana use: trends, patterns and implications. Analytic Series: A17, *DHHS Publication* No. SMA 02 3711. Rockville, MD: Substance Abuse and Mental Health Services Administration, 2002.

19. Gfroerer, JC and Epstein, JF. Marijuana initiates and their impact on future drug abuse treatment need. *Drug and Alcohol Dependence*. 54(3): 229–237, 1999.

20. The National Household Survey on Drug Abuse (NHSDA) Report: Marijuana use among youths. Based on data from the 2000 NHSDA SAMHSA, 2002.

21. Lehman, WE and Simpson, DD. Employee substance use and on the job behaviors. *Journal of Applied Psychology*. 77(3):309-321, 1992.

22. Bolla, KI; Brown, K; Eldreth, D; Tate, K; and Cadet, JL. Dose-related neurocognitive effects of marijuana use. Neurology. 59(9):1337–1343, 2002.

23. A Smoking Gun: The Impact of Cannabis Smoking on Respiratory Health. The British Lung Foundation, 2002.

24. Valois, RF et al. Relationship between number of sexual intercourse partners and selected health risk behaviors among public high school adolescents. *Journal of Adolescent Health*. 25(5): 328–335, 1999. Guo, J; Chung, IJ; Hill, KG; Hawkins, JD; Catalano, RF; and Abbott, RD. Developmental relationships between adolescent substance use and risky sexual behavior in young adulthood. *Journal of Adolescent Health*. 31(4): 354–362, 2002. Graves,

KL and Leigh, BC. The relationship of substance use to sexual activity among young adults in the United States. *Family Planning Perspectives.* 27:1822, 1995. Staton, M et al. Risky sex behavior and substance use among young adults. Health and Social Work. 24(2): 147154, 1999. MARIJUANA MARIJUANA myths & FACTS 29 Whitaker, DJ; Miller, KS; and Clark, LF. Reconceptualizing adolescent sexual behavior: Beyond did they or didn't they? *Family Planning Perspectives.* 32(3): 111–117, 2000. Brook, JS; Balka, EB; and Whiteman, M. The risks for late adolescence of early adolescent marijuana use. American Journal of Public Health. 89(10): 1549–1554, 1999.

25. Rosembaum, E and Kandel, DB. Early onset of adolescent sexual behavior and drug involvement. *Journal of Marriage and the Family.* 52: 783–798, 1990.

26. Guo, J; Chung, IJ; Hill, KG; Hawkins, JD; Catalano, RF; and Abbott, RD. Developmental relationships between adolescent substance use and risky sexual behavior in young adulthood. *Journal of Adolescent Health.* 31(4): 354–362, 2002.

42. Marijuana and Medicine: Assessing the Science Base, Division of Neuroscience and Behavioral Health, Institute of Medicine, 1999.

43. The National Organization for the Reform of Marijuana Laws Home page: http://www.norml.org/
Medical Use: http://norml.org/index.cfm?Group_ID=5441#f4.

72. Unpublished BJS estimates based on the 1997 Survey of Inmates in State and Federal Correctional Facilities, National Archive of Criminal Justice Data. For a public-use copy of the survey data, see http://www.icpsr.umich.edu/NACJD/SISFCF/index.html.

73. *Ibid.*
Prison and Jail Inmates at Midyear 2002, Bureau of Justice Statistics Bulletin, April 2003, NCJ 198877. http://www.ojp.usdoj.gov/bjs/pub/pdf/pjim02.pdf.

74. Prisoners in 2002. Bureau of Justice Statistics, July 2003, NCJ 200248. http://www.ojp.usdoj.gov/bjs/pub/pdf/p02.pdf

75. U.S. Sentencing Commission's 2001 Sourcebook of Federal Sentencing Statistics. Table 33: Primary Drug Type of Offenders Sentenced Under Each Drug Guideline, Fiscal Year 2001. http://www.ussc.gov/ANNRPT/2001/SBTOC01.htm http://www.ussc.gov/ANNRPT/2001/table33.pdf Unpublished figures from the U.S. Sentencing Commission, 2001 Datafile, USSCFY01.

76. Substance Abuse and Mental Health Services Administration, Office of Applied Studies. Treatment Episode Data Set 1992-2000; Table 3.4: Admissions by primary substance of abuse, according to type of service, source of referral to treatment, and planned use of methadone. http://wwwdasis.samhsa.gov/teds00/3.4.htm.

CHAPTER 3: WHAT THE COURTS SAY

EXCERPT FROM "*GONZALES V. RAICH*: IMPLICATIONS FOR PUBLIC HEALTH POLICY," BY SARA ROSENBAUM

1. 125 S. Ct. 2195.
2. 1913 Cal. Stats. ch. 324 §8.
3. Gostin LO. Power, duty and restraint. New York: Oxford University Press; 2003.
4. 21 U.S.C. §§ 801 et. seq.
5. 21 U.S.C. §§ 841(a)(1), 844(a).
6. 125 S. Ct. 2198.
7. Cal. Health & Safety Code § 11362.5.
8. 352 F. 3d 1222 (9th Cir., 2003).
9. 125 S. Ct. 2195, 2201.
10. 514 U.S. 549 (1995).
11. 529 U.S. 598 (2000).
12. 317 U.S. 111 (1942).
13. 125 S. Ct. 2220-2221.
14. 125 S. Ct. 2229.

"IRRATIONAL BASIS: THE LEGAL STATUS OF MEDICAL MARIJUANA," BY REBECCA DRESSER

1. D. Barrett, "Obama Administration Shifts Marijuana Policy," *CNSNews*, March 19, 2009, http://www.cnsnews.com/public / Content/Article.aspx?rsrcid=45277&print=on.
2. Compassionate Use Act, Calif. Health and Safety Code, sec. 11362.5 (West 2007).
3. Medical Marijuana Program Act, Calif. Health and Safety Code, secs. 11362.7–11362.9 (West 2007).

4. County of San Diego v. San Diego NORML, 81 Calif. Rptr. 3d 461 (Calif. Ct. App. 2008).
5. P.J. Cohen, "Medical Marijuana: The Conflict Between Scientific Evidence and Political Ideology," *Utah Law Review* (2009): 35104.
6. Food and Drug Administration, "Inter-Agency Advisory Regarding Claims That Smoked Marijuana Is a Medicine," April 20, 2006, http://www.fda.gov/bbs/topics/NEWS /2006?NEW01362.html.
7. D. Samuels, "Dr. Kush: How Medical Marijuana Is Transforming the Pot Industry," *New Yorker*, July 28, 2008.
8. M. Wohlsen and L. Leff, "'Medical' Marijuana Becomes a Major Economic Force in California," *CNSNews*, July 20, 2009, http:// www.cnsnews.com/public/Content/Article .aspx?rsr-cid=51263&print=on.
9. California Department of Justice, August 25, 2008, http://ag.ca.gov/newsalerts/release .php?id=1601.
10. See J. McKinley, "Marijuana Hotbed Retreats on Medicinal Use," *New York Times*, June 9, 2008.
11. See G. Harris, "F.D.A. to Place New Limits on Prescriptions of Narcotics," *New York Times*, February 10, 2009.

CHAPTER 4: ADVOCACY GROUPS FOR AND AGAINST LEGALIZATION

"LEGALIZATION," BY SAM (SMART APPROACHES TO MARIJUANA)

1. National Survey on Drug Use and Health. (2012). SAMHSA.
2. Kilmer, Beau, Jonathan P. Caulkins, Rosalie Liccardo Pacula, Robert J. MacCoun and Peter H. Reuter. Altered State? Assessing How Marijuana Legalization in California Could Influence Marijuana Consumption and Public Budgets. Santa Monica, CA: RAND Corporation, 2010. http://www.rand.org/pubs/occasional_papers/OP315.
3. Adapted by CESAR from The National Center on Addiction and Substance Abuse at Colombia University (CASA), National Survey of American Attitudes on Substance Abuse XVII: Teens, 2012. Available online athttp://www.casacolumbia.org/upload/2012/20120822teensurvey.pdf.

4. See http://www.taxpolicycenter.org/taxfacts/displayafact. cfm?Docid=399. Also Harwood, H. (2000), Updating Estimates of the Economic Costs of Alcohol Abuse in the United States: Estimates, Update Methods and Data. Report prepared for the National Institute on Alcoholism and Alcohol Abuse.

5. State estimates found at http://www.nytimes.com/2008/08/31/ weekinreview/31saul.html?em; Federal estimates found athttps://www.policyarchive.org/bitstream/handle/10207/3314/ RS20343_20020110.pdf; Also seehttp://www.tobaccofreekids. org/research/factsheets/pdf/0072.pdf; Campaign for Tobacco Free Kids, see "Smoking-caused costs," on p.2.

6. Prohibition: A film by Ken Burns and Lynn Novick. PBS, 2011.

7. "Substance Abuse and Treatment, State and Federal Prisoners, 1997." BJS Special Report, January 1999, NCJ 172871. http:// www.ojp.usdoj.gov/bjs/pub/pdf/satsfp97.pdf

8. Federal Bureau of Investigation (2011). Crime in the United States: 2011. Available from: http://www.fbi.gov/about-us/cjis/ucr/crime-in-the-u.s/2011/ crime-in-the-u.s.-2011

9. Kilmer, Beau, Jonathan P. Caulkins, Brittany M. Bond and Peter H. Reuter. Reducing Drug Trafficking Revenues and Violence in Mexico: Would Legalizing Marijuana in California Help?. Santa Monica, CA: RAND Corporation, 2010. http://www.rand. org/pubs/occasional_papers/OP325.

10. Kilmer, Beau, Jonathan P. Caulkins, Brittany M. Bond and Peter H. Reuter. Reducing Drug Trafficking Revenues and Violence in Mexico: Would Legalizing Marijuana in California Help?. Santa Monica, CA: RAND Corporation, 2010.http:// www.rand.org/pubs/occasional_papers/OP325.

11. MacCoun, R. & Reuter, P. (1997). Interpreting Dutch cannabis policy: Reasoning by analogy in the legalization debate. Science, 278(3): 47–52; cf. de Zwart, W. & van Laar, M. (2001). Cannabis regimes. British Journal of Psychiatry, 178: 574–5.

12. MacCoun, R., calculations using 21 data from EMCDDA 2009 (Tables TDI-1 [new clients], TDI-3 [% with cannabis as primary drug], and GPS-3 [last-year users aged 15-64] and Eurostat-Statistics in Focus (2008; Table 2 [2007 population data]). Found in http://www.rand.org/content/dam/rand/pubs/ working_papers/2010/RAND_WR768.pdf.

13. European Monitoring Center for Drugs and Drug and Addiction. (2011). Drug Policy Profiles Portugal. http://www.emcdda europa.eu/publications/drug-policyprofiles/portugal, p. 24.

GLOSSARY

cannabidiol (CBD)—A compound in cannabis that has medicinal effects with reduced psychoactivity. It does not make users feel high, but it is an effective treatment for debilitating medical conditions.

cannabinoids—Essential chemical compounds that are the active principles in medical marijuana.

cannabis product—A product that contains cannabis or cannabis extracts. In Washington, this designation indicates a product has a THC concentration more than three-tenths of one percent.

controlled substance—A drug or substance included in Schedules I through V of the US Controlled Substance Act (CSA) as classified by federal and state governments.

descheduling—Refers to the federal process of changing marijuana from a Schedule I controlled substance (no medical value, high potential for abuse) to a classification that more accurately reflects how the substance is used.

Drug Enforcement Administration—An agency within the US Department of Justice that enforces federal laws and regulations regarding controlled substances, investigates potential violators, prosecutes the accused, and supervises the seizure and forfeiture assets related to illegal drug trafficking.

edible medical marijuana—Infused product; a product infused with medical marijuana that is meant for oral consumption by way of food, drink, or pill.

Food and Drug Administration—An agency within the US Department of Health and Human Services that governs the oversight of medical products, tobacco, foods, veterinary medicine, global regulatory operations and policy.

Marijuana Enforcement Division (MED)—A division responsible for providing the operational rules for the legal marijuana industry in Colorado.

medical marijuana—Marijuana that is grown and sold according to a state's medical code.

State Licensing Authority—The agency formed for the purpose of regulating and controlling the licensing of the cultivation, manufacture, distribution, sale, and testing of retail marijuana within the state.

strain—Varietals of the marijuana plant, bred for different chemical properties.

support license—A license for an individual who performs duties that support the operations of a marijuana business. A support license indicates the licensee must conduct himself or herself professionally; he or she has restricted authority and reports to a supervisor with an associated key license.

THC—Tetrahydrocannabinol is the chief intoxicant in marijuana.

THCA—Tetrahydrocannabinolic acid is the biosynthetic precursor of tetrahydrocannabinol, the active component of cannabis. When purified, it forms a powder which is unstable in the presence of acids, heat, oxygen, and/or light.

ABOUT THE EDITOR

Anne Cunningham has a PhD in Comparative Literature, and has published articles on women modernist writers and feminist theory. She currently works as an Instructor of English at the University of New Mexico—Taos. She is also a songwriter and performer, and lives with her husband and music partner David Lerner in Arroyo Hondo, NM.

FOR MORE INFORMATION

BOOKS

The Associated Press. *Marijuana Nation: The Legalization of Cannabis Across the USA*. New York, NY: Mango Media Inc., 2015.

Barcott, Bruce. *Weed the People: The Future of Legal Marijuana in America*. New York, NY: Time Books, 2015.

Caulkins, Jonathan, Angela Hawken, Beau Kilmer, and Mark Kleiman. *Marijuana Legalization: What Everyone Needs to Know*. London, UK: Oxford UP, 2012.

Cervantes, Jorge. *The Cannabis Encyclopedia: the Definitive Guide to Cultivation and Consumption of Medical Marijuana*. New York, NY: Van Patten Publishing, 2015.

DeAngelo, Steve. *The Cannabis Manifesto*. Berkeley, CA: North Atlantic Books, 2015.

Fine, Doug. *Hemp Bound: Dispatches From the Front Lines of the Next Agricultural Revolution*. White River Junction, VT: Chelsea Green Publishing, 2014.

Fine, Doug. *Too High to Fail: Cannabis and the New Green Economic Revolution*. New York, NY: Gotham, 2013.

Grissler, Jeff. *Marijuana Business: How to Open and Successfully Run a Marijuana Dispensary and Grow Facility*. New York, NY: Marijuana Business Books Publishing, 2014.

Hagseth, Christian. *Big Weed: An Entrepreneur's High-Stakes Adventures in the Budding Legal Marijuana Business*. New York, NY: St. Martin's Press, 2015.

Holland, Julie. *The Pot Book: A Complete Guide to Cannabis—Its Role in Medicine, Politics, Science, and Culture*. Rochester, NY: Park Street Press, 2010.

Martin, Alyson and Nushin Rashidian. *A New Leaf: The End of Cannabis Prohibition*. New York, NY: The New Press, 2014.

Walker, Jon. *After Legalization: Understanding the Future of Marijuana*. Washington, DC: FDL Writers Foundation, 2014.

WEBSITES

The Drug Policy Alliance's Marijuana Legalization and Regulation Factsheet
drugpolicy.org/marijuana-legalization-and-regulation
> The Drug Policy Alliance is another pro-marijuana reform group. Accurate information and arguments for legalization touching on increased tax revenue, reduced racial injustice, and expanded personal liberty can be found here, as well as an "Ask the Expert" section.

Governing Magazine's State Marijuana Laws Map
www.governing.com/gov-data/state-marijuana-laws-map-medical-recreational.html
> This is a neutral site that provides up-to-date information about marijuana laws on a state-by-state basis. It also includes relevant articles, election and law enforcement data, and commentary.

The National Organization for the Reform of Marijuana Laws
norml.org
> NORML is the most established advocacy group working toward marijuana reform and the website is a great resource for state-by-state marijuana laws as well as current news and developments on the topic.

Smart Approaches to Marijuana
learnaboutsam.org
> SAM (Smart Approaches to Marijuana) is an organization that opposes legalization and favors decriminalization and other measures that reduce the volume of marijuana cases straining the criminal justice system. Their site contains much useful information, with a key focus on the prevention of a powerful, corporatized marijuana lobby they call Big Tobacco 2.0.

Why Legalize Marijuana: Supporting the Legalization of Marijuana Use
whylegalizemarijuana.com
> This marijuana reform site has links to other leading pro-legalization groups, a news roundup on their sidebar, as well as books, articles, and essays.

INDEX